Simply your life with the Clutter Cutter guide to Freedom

by **Lina Visconti**

The Clutter Cutter Guide
to Freedom
by Lina Visconti

Copyright © 2002 by Lina Visconti

published by
Lina Visconti o/a
TM Publications
9251 Yonge Street, Unit 121
Richmond Hill, Ontario L4C 9T3

Library of Congress
Cataloging-in-Publication Data
on file with the publisher
Clutter Cutter Guide
I S B N   0-9684391-5-2

© Cover design by Lynn Waghorne
© Illustrations by Roseanna Pullara
© Photographs by Lina Visconti, Carmen Visconti

Technical Design and layout by Tom Mallioras

First edition 2002

Printed by Webcom Limited, Toronto, Canada.

for
Tomaso
Thank You!

Table of Contents

Acknowledgements

I would like to thank
Rick, Maryanne, John Mark
for their encouragement and patience.
Mom and Dad *for their words of wisdom.*
Lidia Kafieh, Robert Kafieh, John Kafieh,
Josette Turco, Carmen Visconti,
Jennifer Volpe, Suzanne Volpe, Al Lau
for their enthusiasm and support.
Tom Mallioras,
for his technical brilliance and support
Lynn Waghorne *for the beautiful cover design.*
Roseanna Pullara *for her clever illustrations.*
Lyn Alcock, Yvonne Sciavilla, Olivera Koledin
for editing
and a special thanks to
Barry Birnberg, Joshua Zuchter,
and David Leonhardt
for their insightfull contributions.

Introduction

Early in 1997 things were not going at all well for me. I had
challenges in almost every area of my life and I really
believed that it was because I was 40 something. Being that
age and not feeling it, pushed me into a deep sense of
denial. But seriously, the problems were real. I was having
identity crises, my kids were growing up, I needed a career
change, we were experiencing financial problems and my
marriage was suffering. To top it all off I was involved in
more than my share of car accidents. I think that 7 accidents
in a two-year period are a little excessive to say the least.
They were all what I would call freak accidents. One time
I was making a left on a busy road and a lady ran a red light
and hit me from behind throwing me into the ongoing traffic. It appeared that she fell asleep at the wheel. Fortunately
no one got hurt. Another time I was driving a new car, drove
over a bump and the air bag blew up. Two young boys came
running over and thought it was very funny. When the air
bag popped open it hit my face and all you could see on the
deflating air bag was two big red lipstick marks.

Late June in 1997, my sister called from her home in Naples
Park Florida. She had heard I was having a rough time and
made me an offer I could not refuse. My sister is a muralist
and a very good one at that. She has been featured in some
of the top Architecture and design magazines in South
Florida. Apparently she had a few big contracts to complete
and needed a little help. She offered to pay for my trip and
commented "If you are going to be stressed and depressed
you might as well do it down here. You can watch the dol-

1

phins swimming in the Gulf and help me at the same time."
I left early the next week.

In Florida, everyone I ran into was either retired, wealthy or
running a prosperous business. I was trying to be positive
but all I could think about was my situation at home and it
still looked pretty pathetic. One day just out of the blue my
sister asked if I had ever thought of practicing Fenga Chewy
"fenga what?" I asked. She explained that this was an
ancient Chinese art that could help me balance my life. She
went on to explain that if you moved your stuff around and
faced certain directions you could invite prosperity into
your life. I did remember reading articles on some Chinese
practice that claimed to do that. "It also has to do with
using the elements and colours of nature in your home." At
this point I became curious. She went on to explain that
many of the top designers and architects were getting into
it. "Are you into it?" I asked. "Of course I am, always have
been, except I never knew what it was called". My sister's
artwork always reflected the natural colours, lines and balance of nature. I thought to myself that the whole idea of
working with the laws of nature wasn't exactly a new concept. Sounded like common sense to me.

On the way home from work that evening we stopped into
the Barns and Noble Book store in search of books on this
Chinese Art of Placement. There were only three books on
the shelf. I skimmed through the books and decided on one
written by Lillian Too. The other two books seemed a little
complicated and long winded. I just wanted something that
could tell me how I could use this art in my own personal

2

life. One of the first things I learned is that the art was called Feng Shui. Feng sounds like tongue and Shui sounds like sway. My sister insisted on buying the book for me. She had a strong feeling that it would bring me luck.

Call it luck, call it destiny or call it coincidence but that same evening I was reading the local paper and noticed an advertisement for a Feng Shui workshop that was being held on the weekend. Apparently, the instructor giving the workshop was from California and a local Woman's club invited her to Florida to teach this workshop. Without hesitation I called and registered both my sister and I in the class. It hadn't occurred to me to ask if she were available after all she would be the one driving me since there was virtually no other way to get there. Was it a coincidence that she just happened to have that Saturday off? Things were clicking into place. Was there a message here for me? Was this the reason I came to Florida?

The workshop started off a little weird. The instructor walked into the room, correction, she floated into the room dangling a crystal in her hand. She had long wavy hair with two white streaks on the sides and she wore a long flowing skirt with beads hanging from the waste. She reminded me of a hippie, actually I would say a new age hippie. Although I was not involved in any type of new age movement I most definitely had an open mind and was quite curious about what she had to say. I shared my excitement with forty other students who were just as eager to find out how Feng Shui could influence their lives.

The workshop was based on concepts centred around Black Hat Sect, a school of thought that focuses on a New Age/Spiritual type of Feng Shui. We were taught that a Guru introduced this type of Feng Shui to the west from Malaysia. The school of Black Hat was based in California. Some of the ideas seemed a little far-fetched but I kept an open mind. About half way into the workshop the instructor began to talk about the five elements in nature and how they represented cycles of harmony and conflict and that it was important to balance the elements and make sure that they flowed in their creative order. She went on to explain that these elements were not just a physical elements but that they were also associated with compass direction, colour and energy. That is when it hit me. This was it! All of sudden my past, future and present collided at the same time and I knew that I was exactly where I should be and that this was my path. Feng Shui is what I needed to get my life back in order and once more I would be teaching this and it would be my career. My heart started pounding and I became very excited. I remember elbowing my sister and saying. "This is it, this is what I want to do! I can teach this!" "How can you know you will teach this when you don't even know much about it?" she replied. "It doesn't matter - I just know".

Have you ever had a moment or insight that felt so good and so right that in one single moment everything changes? I knew that my life was about to change for the better. The last hour of the seminar focused on how clutter blocks and stagnates the flow of positive energy. I kept thinking of the piles of clutter I had at home. It all made so much sense!

4

During the remainder of my stay in Florida I cruised all four corners of the Internet. Read as much as I could and sent away for information on courses. I became an insatiable sponge, talking, eating and dreaming Feng Shui. Before I knew it was time for me to go home. The flight home went very quickly as I spent the whole time reading about Feng Shui and making notes. There were many things that seemed strange, outdated and not at all practical but deep down inside I knew that I would figure it all out and that Feng Shui would change my life.

Once I arrived I expressed to my family my new found direction in life. My kids thought I was weird and my husband raised his eyebrows and said "It sounds interesting." I told them that the first thing we needed to do was to get rid of the clutter. I instructed everyone to get their stuff ready and scheduled a garage sale for the following weekend. We had so much stuff that we ended up having five garage sales to rid ourselves of all the junk we had collected over the years. We sold old furniture, toys, clothing and tons of other stuff. Whatever we couldn't sell we either threw out or gave to charity. It was a wonderful cleansing experience both on a physical and mental level. We all felt a little lighter to rid ourselves of all the excess stuff that crowded our garage basement and cupboards. We calculated that we sold approx $1000. worth of stuff. We used the money to pay some of our overdue bills. Things were getting better already.

There was not much happening with Feng Shui in Toronto. There were only one or two people who were practicing, one of which offered an introductory course. What I really wanted was an intensive training program. I received a package in the mail from a company in the USA that offered an intensive training program for Feng Shui Practitioners. I needed to borrow the money to cover the fee and hotel. Without hesitation I enrolled and in October I drove to Detroit for a four-day training held at the University of Michigan. I completed the course, took the exam and became a certified Feng Shui Practitioner before the end of the year.

I spent a great deal of time reading at the library and one day the librarian approached me and asked if I was interested in conducting a special interest workshop. He took notice of the fact that I was constantly looking up information and reading about Feng Shui. I said sure, figuring that I could handle a small group. Four weeks later I found myself speaking to a full room of 33 anxious students, eager to learn more about Feng Shui. I was surprised at how much knowledge I was able to share with them. From that workshop I booked two consultations and a lecture for a local Newcomers Club. Things started to move quickly after that and almost on a daily basis I was booking consultations, talks and workshops.

The only challenge I had was organizing my material in such a way that it would come across as simple and easy to follow. Feng Shui was an ancient art that was developed in China thousands of years ago. Much of the information available was outdated and not very practical. After sorting through all my research I realized that the material I had accumulated was a blueprint for a book that needed to be written. Without giving it a second thought I jumped in with both feet and came up with my first book entitled "Seven Step Feng Shui". I self published it in 1998 and much to everyone's surprise the first run sold out before the end of the year. In 1999 I published "Feng Shui Going With The Flow" and then in 2000 I released a new revised edition of "Seven Step Feng Shui". Later that year, I also produced a video called "Simply Feng Shui".

In the year 2000 I began to notice that during my Feng Shui Basics class, students would become quite anxious whenever I mentioned clutter. I would speak about how clutter blocks the energy flow in your space and how each and every item is attached to you by a thread. Whenever the subject of clutter would come up it would prompt great discussion within the class. I would hear comments like "I have so much stuff that our house is too small", "clutter just keeps on accumulating" and questions like "how do we get rid of the stuff and what do we do with it?" This became quite a hot spot in the Feng Shui Classes and since it was so hard for students to move past that section I decided to schedule a separate class focussed on how to Eliminate Clutter. Both the Feng Shui and clutter classes were always full. In fact, there was a waiting list for my next class. What was interesting about these classes is that women were dragging in their husbands and parents were coming with their teenage kids. Everyone from stay-at-home moms, teachers, small business owners to corporate professionals attended the workshops. It wasn't unusual to have lawyers in the class but one day a Judge showed up. Everyone seemed to have too much clutter in their lives.

My students would share how they had difficulty dealing with the accumulation of stuff in their homes and I could see the amount of frustration, stress and confusion it was causing them just to talk about it. I did dozens of surveys and the results were always the same. The fact was, that almost everyone had clutter and everyone felt out-of-control. They would clear it away and be happy for a while and then it would start piling up again. For a short time, I changed the workshop name to "Cluttertherapy" because I found that all people wanted to do was share their clutter stories with others.

In my own personal life, I discovered that eliminating clutter was only a short-term solution. I invested in courses, books and storage units but no matter how much stuff I got rid of there was always more to fill its place.

I spent days and months researching clutter. One thing kept leading into another and it seemed that the more I read the more confused I was. One day I would be reading about the psychology of clutter the next day I would be reading about consumerism, advertising and patterns of economic growth. Things were getting a little out of-control and my mind was so overloaded with information that I was ready to give up. I knew that these areas had to be connected but I had to somehow find a way of simplifying it in my mind before I could ever think about putting it down on paper. Finally I concluded the following;

Advertising is the tool that is used to fuel Consumerism. Consumerism is a term used to describe people that buy and use stuff. That would be us. Advertising is designed to create the need, want and desire to acquire anything and everything no matter what the cost to the Consumer. We are led to believe that if we buy we will be happy, healthy and prosperous. We buy with this in mind only to find that these things don't make us happy. We keep on buying thinking that the next bigger and better product will make us happy but it doesn't. So we just keep on buying and accumulating stuff to the point of over-consumption. Then we end up with too much stuff or clutter. Clutter is actually the end result of how materialistic we have become. As the clutter accumulates it creates problems on many different levels. It affects us on a physical, mental and emotional level. It affects our quality of life from the family to the community and the environment. It is making us feel sick, stressed out, overworked, empty and off balance.

The Clutter Cutter Guide is not just about getting rid of stuff, organizing and beautifying. It goes much deeper than that. You need to develop an understanding of why and how you clutter. Cutting Clutter from your life is an attitude and a way of life. It's about redefining your goals to reflect your true values. It's about making conscious choices as to what you need to sustain your life rather than buying and choosing things based on what commercials tell you.

We all need to take back control of our lives so that we can lead a balanced and happy life. This means clearing the clutter on both a physical and mental level so. Simplifying your life and freeing yourself from the strings that bind you is a wonderful cleansing experience. And so I offer you a way to Simplify Your Life with The Clutter Cutters Guide to Freedom.

How to use this book

The Clutter Cutter Guide has been broken down into seven easy-to-follow bite size pieces or chapters. I have also included insightful and thought provoking essays, letters and quotes submitted to me by students, friends, professionals and other authors. Included in these words of wisdom is a speech written by a 10-year-old boy who innocently speaks about thoughtless adults who in their quest for bigger and better create havoc on the way to school. I suggest that the first thing you do is to flip through and familiarize yourself with all of the contents of this book.

Chapter One defines the many aspects of clutter and how it affects us on all levels. Check the survey at the end of the chapter to see if you can identify with the results.

Chapter Two answers the question - How did we get so cluttered? It paints a pretty clear picture of how things got so out-of-control. You may want to read through this section a few times. It covers things like modern technology, advertising and consumerism. Do you have Clutter? Take a few minutes to do the Clutter Cutter Quiz at the end of this chapter, if only for a laugh.

Chapter Three is designed to help you create a plan of action. It's important to be clear on what it is that you are trying to accomplish. Exactly what are you making room for? Why do you want to clear your clutter? Read the Goal Setting section and jot down a few short term goals by using the Goal Chart . If time is what is holding you back read the section on TIME and try doing a TIME LOG. You may be surprised to find out how many hours a day you waste. There are dozens of tips on how to clear up calendar clutter by properly utilizing a TO-DO-LIST.

Clearing clutter is the first step you can take towards living a balanced life and creating good Feng Shui in your home. For those of you who have not read my other books entitled Seven Step Feng Shui and Feng Shui, Going With The Flow I have included a section that highlights FENG SHUI and how to use the Pa Kua Grid. This is a map that is placed over your floor plan to identify the areas of life that correspond to eight compass directions. This is a great tool that will help you to identify which areas of your life are being blocked by the clutter in your space.

I have identified clutter into two main categories, Space and Paper Clutter. Chapter Four and Five will give you the tips, ideas, charts and checklists designed to help you cut the clutter out of your space. These two chapters are set up so you can easily find what you are looking for, without having to read through paragraphs of information.

Chapter Six is on Environmental Clutter. My surveys indicated that many people were concerned about what to do with clutter once they removed it from their homes. This will give you an idea of what happens to your garbage once it leaves the curbside. You will find some interesting ideas on recycling and reusing and disposing of unwanted goods and garbage. You may be surprised to see how much stuff we waste as well as the effects it has on the environment.

Finally, Chapter Seven is on how to simplify your Life so you can free yourself from clutter once and for all. This chapter isn't meant to convince you to go and live in a forest and become a minimalist. The focus of this chapter is to provide you with some insight into the idea of living a simpler life style. To do this you need to re-consider and re-evaluate what really makes you happy. The tips and suggestions will help you find the freedom to get back control of your life.

Our stuff is making us feel out-of-control!

Chapter One

What is Clutter?

Merriam Webster's Dictionary defines clutter as
verb - to run in disorder   noun - a crowded or confused
mass or collection of things

Most dictionaries agree that clutter is stuff or things. We can safely say that we are dealing with materialist possessions. The accumulation of all these possessions and the need to constantly acquire them has certainly impacted the way we live.

The first and most obvious clutter is Physical Clutter. Physical clutter includes items and objects that basically take up space so I call this SPACE CLUTTER. The other category is listed as PAPER CLUTTER. Although it still takes up space, paper clutter is such a huge challenge that it needed to be addressed separately.

15

Space Clutter

Space Clutter is the stuff that takes up space in your cupboards, closets, garages attics and bathrooms. It's the stuff you own the stuff you collect and the stuff you keep buying. Stuff that you don't use, don't need and stuff you get tired of. It's the stuff you collect and things that you buy to make you look and feel good. It's the gadgets and technological wonders that promise to make your life easier and more efficient. It's the stuff that malls are made of. What best describes our obsession with stuff is the commercial where one woman says to a depressed women, "sister you need shopping therapy", and they go to the mall and buy all kinds of useless stuff.

Paper Clutter

Paper Clutter is the junk mail, email, letters, boxes, wrapping paper, cards, books, magazines and newspapers that keep piling up. It's all the bits and pieces of information that you can't seem to rid yourself of. It's the recipes you never use or the articles that you'll never read. Paper clutter lives in your current files and in your stored files. This by far is one of the most troublesome clutter categories to deal with.

Processed Clutter

We are constantly buying and consuming fast-foods. Our cupboards and freezers are filled quick easy microwavable dishes so we can eat and run. Fast food chains are popping up on ever corner filling a need for those late workers who don't make it home on time for dinner. Our bodies are being filled with unhealthy processed food resulting in diseases such as obesity and colon cancer.

Clutter has managed to penetrate our whole existence. We seem to be accumulating clutter everywhere we look, our homes, garages and even our cars. In addition to the physical clutter there is a another kind of clutter, one that can be found in every hour of every day.

Time Clutter

Time Clutter is the clutter on our calendars, date books and our to-do lists. We have so much stuff to do that we rush around like rats in a maze from one place to the other. We are constantly complaining about having no time. Comments like "where does the time go?" and "I have so much to do and so little time" are part of our every day dialogue. "Time clutter" may not be an accurate phrase because time is not a material thing. It is, however, a valuable commodity that cannot be controlled. Time keeps moving forward no matter what we do. No one, and certainly not I, can promise you more time. The section on time in Chapter Three will help you recognize and evaluate what you do with your time and how you can make better use of it. Almost everyone I know complains that they have no time, meanwhile they are spending their time running around shopping, buying and maintaining stuff that they don't even use.

Environmental Clutter

Clutter can also be found in the air we breathe, the water we drink and in the food we eat. This type of clutter is polluting our environments and our bodies. For the most part it cannot be seen, but sometimes we can catch a glimpse of it hovering over our cities and floating in our lakes.

There is so much toxic stuff infiltrating the air we breathe and the water we drink. Asthma, in young children and adults is becoming a growing concern. Pollution is creating chaos in our entire environment. Along with pollutants caused by factories and air conditioners there is the seepage from land fill sites and let's not forget the pollution caused by cars, trucks, buses, trains and planes. The ozone layer is being depleted while clutter is filling our minds and bodies and our homes.

Clutter is energy
Everything is energy, people, plants, rocks, dirt, water, soil and sand including emotions, feelings, thoughts, dreams, desires and fears. Everything vibrates at different frequencies and co-exists at the same time. Everything is linked together. Energy can be transformed from one form to another but can neither be created nor destroyed. It follows the cycle attraction and repulsion.

We are connected to our clutter
Everything in our home is energetically connected to us. Depending on a person's state of mind things can have a positive or negative effect. The negative or positive state lasts only a moment but the observer can choose to hold on to it. It's a scientific fact that when this transpires the energy must change into another state. When this happens we can become physically ill or tired because it takes energy to hold on to that emotion. Since childhood we are taught to hold on to our emotions and to suppress our feelings.

Psychological Clutter
Pictures, items and objects can conjure up emotions simply by looking at them. Lets say that you go out and purchase a painting of a beautiful woman, sitting alone in a garden. The woman is in deep thought and looks very sad. You like the picture because you can identify with it. It reminds you of how you feel. You take it home, hang it on your wall. Soon you forget that it is there, but each time you walk past it, you connect with those initial feelings of sadness..

In the book, "Life Energy and the Emotions" John Diamond explains the effects that pictures can have on people. He explains how the emotional states associated with each of the energy channels in the body, are affected from the feelings and energy you get after observing a photo. For example one might be tested as weak in the heart meridian after looking at a certain photo, or weak in the liver meridian after looking at another photo.

There is a definite connection between your internal state and external environment. It is a well-documented fact that we react to and often mirror our surroundings. The Chinese art of Feng Shui, has been used for over 5000 years to correct and encourage the flow of energy or chi within an environment. Attracting positive chi can create good health, wealth and healthy relationships while the flow of negative energy can create disharmony in all those areas. In the book, "The Power of Place" by Winifred Gallagher, Psychologist, Peter Suedfeld states that "we can become over or under stimulated by our environment" meaning there is too much or too little chi.

We are all trying to live like "super humans" trying to do everything we can, as fast as we can. Our brains are on overload, taking in information and trying to process it at record speed. We don't want to wait for anything, we want things fast, we think fast and move fast. Some people loose their minds trying to do so much so fast.

When we look or think about our stuff we are constantly reminded of things we need to do, and things we need to finish. We think about the phone calls we need to make and the letters we need to write. We are pulled in so many different directions that it makes us feel out-of-control. We are overcome with feelings of guilt, fear, indecisiveness and most of all procrastination and we are realizing that perhaps, it's the clutter that's making us feel like we are living in chaos.

For the past two years I've surveyed students from at least twenty of my "Eliminating Clutter" and "Cluttertherapy" workshops. After reviewing the first few hundred surveys I noticed that the answers to most of the questions were the same. In my opinion, the survey below represents a true picture of how clutter is affecting our society. Many of the students indicated their clutter concerns were mostly centred within their home. Others indicted that their biggest problem was paper clutter, overloaded day timers and calendars (Time clutter)

In all of my clutter classes I pass out a short survey that asks a few simple questions. My quest is to discover what it is about clutter that attracts so many people to my workshops.

The survey below is based on 400 students who attended my classes between Jan 2001 and April 2002. I still hand out the survey to my students but the answers are generally the same.

Clutter Cutter Survey

SAMPLE taken from Jan 2001 to June 2002
TOTAL SURVEYED - 400 workshop attendees.
AGE/SEX Ages 30-60, Male and female of various cultural backgrounds and occupations.

1. What do you hope to learn from this workshop?
a) Simple & inexpensive ideas/tips   48 %
b) Motivation   25
c) Misc.   20
d) General Information   7

2. What is your biggest clutter challenge?
a) Stuff   57.5 %
b) Paper   35
c) Misc.   7.5

3. How does clutter make you feel?
a) Stressed   35 %
b) Out-of-control   25
c) Tired/disorganized   13
d) Overloaded   12
e) Stuck   7.5
f) Chaotic/unfulfilled/misc   5

g) None of the above   2.5

4. Why do you think you have so much clutter?
  a) No time to clear it   34.5%
  b) Holding on just in case   21
  c) Holding on to the past   16
  d) Consumerism/materialistic   13
  e) Procrastinate/guilt/lazy/fear 6
  f) Other peoples stuff   5
  g) Misc.   2.5
  h) None of the above   2

5. Removing clutter from my life will make me feel….
  a) Free   32 %
  b) Happy   26
  c) In control/organized   19.5
  d) De-stressed/relaxed   15
  e) Make my spouse happy   5
  f) Creative/Misc   2.5

Home is a mirror reflection of you

Chapter Two

How did we get so cluttered?

The way we were

Back in the cave days, home was a place that provided protection against danger and shelter from the elements. For the cave man, possessions consisted of the clothing on their back and a few hunting tools. They would hunt for their food and utilized every part of their catch for clothing and tools. Moving from cave to cave was easy because they were able to carry their possessions in one hand. They never became attached to any cave in particular because home was simply where they laid their tools.

As man became more "civilized", home became a more permanent dwelling. The longer he stayed in the same place the more stuff he accumulated. Evidence of this can be seen today in every level of our society. Homeless people literally carry all of their belongings with them from place to place, whereas the affluent hire a moving van to transport their possessions.

As time went on larger homes were built to accommodate the size of a family and all of their stuff. Today people buy a bigger home that is big enough to not just house their family but also to store all of their stuff. It is not unusual to hear people complain that they don't have enough room for their stuff.

Modern Technology
As we progressed our lives became more structured. Life started to move a little quicker. Modern technology came along and soon all kinds of products and gadgets were invented claiming to make life easier. Because most of the day is spent working so people wanted to maximize the time spent at home. Modern technology soon began to focus on products that provided entertainment, convenience and pleasure. All of these things promised to make life easier.

Today, most homes have at least one television, radio and phone in very room. In addition to a home phone just about everyone carries a cell phone or some other type of electronic gadget. All these electronic gadgets were developed to help us communicate faster.

Imagine if a highly advanced being from another planet dropped in to see how we live. What would be going through his head?

"Hummm interesting species. They work hard to earn money, buy lots of stuff that they don't need , accumulate it, store it, dust it, look at it and then they go off and buy more. They buy little things in big packages, use them a few times and then throw them away. Strange, why they would throw away something that is still good. Then they run out and buy the same thing again with some minor modifications. At this rate they are consuming more than this planet can absorb. Rather perplexing why such a species would work so hard to destroy the very planet that sustains their life."

Take a look at yourself through the eyes of an alien. Last time I did that I found myself uttering the words "beam me up Scotty".

Welcome to the material world

Madonna said it in her song " I am a material girl, living in a material world", a song that reflected a sign of the times. The song was from the 80's but the concept still remains the same. We are living in a material world and living a material life. Who we are is judged by what we have or don't have. We live in a time where citizens are referred to as "consumers." Our lives are based on an insatiable desire to acquire possessions. To live is to buy and to buy is to live. Most of us are imbedded so deeply into this lifestyle that it almost feels normal. We are running around in circles working, buying, paying and owing and then doing over again and again. Life today is like living on a carousel. We are going so fast that we are afraid to get off for fear that we may never get back on. How did things get so crazy? There are a number of factors that contributed to the con- sumer-oriented world we live in. First lets look at our own habits.

We buy more than we need

Take a look in your kitchen cupboards. We keep stockpil- ing boxes and cans of food that we will probably never consume. The cupboards are filled with all kinds of plates, utensils and gadgets that we never use and we hang on to them thinking that someday we may find a use for them.

It takes space to store all of the stuff we accumulate so we are constantly upgrading our living quarters and trying to figure out how to make more space. Stuff fills our homes and spills over into the garage, the basement and the attic. It's not unusual to see a three car garage filled with clutter not cars. It is not unusual to hear someone say that we need a bigger house because we have so much stuff. How many people do you know that actually park their car in the garage? Most use it for storage, after all you can never have enough storage space. Most families today own more than one car.

We want everything we see

Thanks to advertising we are constantly being bombarded with all of the latest products. We are tempted with the newest tools, gadgets, fashionable clothing, novelty items, decorative items, artwork, furniture and cars and we want them all.

We want everything right away

The going attitude seems to be "Why wait?" We live in the now, in the moment, so why not get it right away? Tomorrow it may be too late. Buy now and pay later. Just take out the plastic and bingo - it's yours.

We buy because we feel we deserve it

We believe that we work so hard and deserve to have anything we want. It's our right to live like the rich and famous. It is so easy, all we have to do is buy the same stuff they buy and we can be just like them.

Our possessions are us

Our possessions have become a way of defining ourselves. We let the world know who we are by what we have "I am the guy driving the silver BMW or "I am the one wearing the blue Armani. We boast about how we have the newest and the best as if we are competing for a prize.

Our success is judged by our stuff

People judge us by what we wear, what we drive, where we live, the clothes we wear and the stuff we own. Everyday you hear people saying things like "He must be making good money, look at what he drives" and "He has a gold credit card he is probably loaded".

There are people who take exotic holidays, drive fancy cars, own huge homes, wear designer clothes, carry limitless credit cards and have high profile jobs. On the surface it may appear that they are living a prosperous life, but the truth is, they are one pay cheque away from being bankrupt.

Keeping up with the Jones'

As outdated as it may sound we are still trying to keep up with the Jones'. As soon as we hear that someone has something new and better we begin our quest to acquire it. The mentality is that if they have it, then we should have it too.

Stuff Happens

Along with our desire to acquire possessions we tend to accumulate stuff for a variety of other reasons. Breakups, second time around marriages, illness, accidents, and living with others are to blame for some of the excess. As our parents pass on they leave us with a house full of stuff that they accumulated. We like to collect things and hang on to them just in case or for nostalgic reasons. Unforeseen circumstances often result in a need for friends and relatives using your place for storage. Children grow up, leave home and then come back each time leaving stuff behind. We often hold on to stuff because it reminds us of the past, and that, can be difficult to let go of.

Along with the regular reasons for holding on to stuff there may be more complex reasons for accumulating and holding on to stuff. In her book "House as a Mirror of Self," author Clare Marcus Cooper, explores some of the deep rooted reasons of how self is expressed through the house and the objects in it.

What is consumerism?

Merriam Webster Dictionary Definition
Consumerism noun - the promotion of the consumer's interest, the theory that an increasing consumption of goods is

economically desirable and a preoccupation with and an inclination toward the buying of consumer goods
What is the consumer? Consumer noun - one that utilizes economic goods
The definition above is an updated version of the 1947 Oxford Dictionary which defined as "make away with and use up" the word excessive is also used in the definition. The consumer is the person who is wasting and using up.

The bigger the car the better!
Along with the big house we drive big cars. Monster trucks, SUV's and Mini Vans. They seem to be getting bigger and funkier. They remind me of a the toy trucks that kids used to play with. It's understandable if you have a very large family. Owning your own business and having to cart stuff around is also a good reason for owning a SUV. Some people buy a large vehicle for reasons of safety, but research has indicated that larger vehicles are not necessarily the safest during accidents. The next time you are in a traffic jam take a look at all the SUV's around you and count how many passengers are in them. If you are lucky, you may even get to see one with a portable TV in it. Some of these big SUV's look like portable living rooms. SUV's are responsible for large percentage of pollution caused by automobile fumes? Most of these vehicles are so huge that they have difficulty getting into a parking space and drivers of these big vehicles block traffic in all directions while trying to negotiate a parking spot. When we drive behind them they block off our view that it becomes

difficult to see where you are going and you end up missing your turnoff. It is strange that when these SUV's are advertised, they are often pictured in natural settings like a long dirt road or on a scenic country style. They are advertised as the car to buy when you want to get away and take the family camping or simply go for a drive. They fail to tell you: First of all, you won't have the time because you will be busy working extra hours to pay for it. Secondly, good luck trying to get away since there is so much traffic on the road it will take you a while to get there, once you get there, others will be right behind you with their SUV's.

Then there is the sports car. Advertisers suggest that if we buy the car we can fly across an open highway with the love of our life sitting next to us. Sounds like a wonderful dream. Just how often will your love let you drive that fast? The other trouble with fancy sports cars is that owners are in constant fear that someone will scratch or steel it from them, so parking it in a regular spot is out of the question.

I know many people who own a family car, sports car and another car to go to work with. I can just imagine the costs involved in insurance, gas and maintaining all these vehicles.
Sarah B, age 42 Toronto, Ont.

Although consumerism is a fairly new term it relates to using up and wasting of goods with the words "economically desirable" and pre-occupation" as well as "the inclination towards the buying of consumer goods."

Our pre-occupation with shopping and buying goods has been engineered so perfectly that we are compelled to buy stuff whether or not we need it. We are being inundated with thousands of messages a day telling us that we need products if we want to be happy. Advertisements tell us that we need products to make us look and feel young, attractive and successful. We are told that we need to use products that will disinfect our hands, bodies our water and the air. We are being told that we need products to make our hair, nails and teeth look perfect. We are being told that we need the newest the best and the most updated technology in order to keep up with the times. "Told" is rather a weak word to use." convinced" is a better word or maybe "brainwashed". The machine that is doing this to us is none other than the monster I call "Advertising".

Advertising
Merriam Webster's Dictionary Definition
Advertise verb- to make something known or to notify and to make public and generally known, to announce publicly especially by a printed notice or broadcast, to call public attention to especially be emphasizing desirable qualities so as to arouse a desire to buy or patronize

This monster is everywhere we turn. It's on TV, radio, newspapers, magazines, billboards, subways, trains, and airplanes and on the clothes we wear. It is seeping into our very social fabric and has even managed to sneak into our schools and places of worship. We have been influenced so deeply that we are convinced that the material goods we use, wear drive and own, define us. We are so convinced of this that we ourselves have become human billboards. We wear clothing with designer names on them and lately we even are re-designing ourselves to be new and improved through cosmetic surgery which is in itself advertising for surgeons. Consider this "do you like my new nose" or "what do you think of my new breasts". Yes, these two are products that we wear proudly. Cosmetic surgery and enhancements are no different from being told that we need to update our car or our computer with a new better faster model. Even though there was nothing wrong with it in the first place.

Judging by the recent interest in de-clutter books, talks and workshops it's obvious that everyone is concerned about the amount of clutter they have accumulated. Everyone seems to be waking up and asking themselves if it's all worth it. It costs money to buy and keep stuff and it takes time to upkeep it as well. More and more people are beginning to feel that things have gotten out-of-control. Maybe people are catching on and realizing that advertisers are selling us a false sense of happiness and once more they keep convincing us to buy and charge so much that we feel like we are loosing control of lives. Our family and social life is suffering and things things feel so off balance.

Is clutter affecting your life? Take the Clutter Cutter Quiz below and decide for yourself.

CLUTTER CUTTER QUIZ

1. How do you feel when you get unexpected guests?
   a) Great! I love guests!
   b) I usually need to clear off a place for them to sit.
   c) I don't answer the door.

2. What condition is your garage in?
   a) Excellent, I park my car in it.
   b) I need to clear away stuff when I park.
   c) Our garage is so full, there's no room for a car.

3. Do you ever have trouble finding your keys?
   a) I always know where they are.
   b) It only takes me twenty minutes to find them.
   c) I've invested in an electronic key locator.

4. Do you enjoy all and use of your stuff?
   a) I have little and enjoy everything I own.
   b) I like most of my stuff, the rest I keep just in case.
   c) I have so much stuff I need a bigger house.

5. What is in your handbag at this moment?
   a) A wallet, lipstick and keys/ I only carry a wallet.
   b) A wallet, receipts, 2 lipsticks and nail polish.
   c)Tons of receipts, makeup bag, papers and socks.

6. How do you feel about passengers in your car?

a) I enjoy having a passenger in my car.

b) No problem! I just throw everything on the back

c) It can never happen there is no room in my car.

7. How long would it take you to find a stamp and an envelope?

a) 30 seconds, I know exactly where they are!

b) If lucky I might find some under the papers on my desk.

c) I can never find them, so I just run out and buy more.

8. Do you pay your bills on time?

a) I pay them as soon as they come in.

b) I go through them once a month.

c) They usually call me to remind me to pay my bill.

9. How long does it take you to get dressed in the morning?

a) 5 minutes.

b) I can never decide what to wear, I have too many choices.

c) I don't have a thing to wear I need to go shopping.

10. Did you get a lot done today?

a) I completed most of my to-do list.

b) I didn't get much done because of interruptions.

c) It was a complete waste of a day I don't remember what I did.

11. Do you have a good savings plan?

a) Yes! I find any way I can to save money.

b) I make decent money and save a little.
c) I don't save much, however I own lots of
expensive stuff.

Check your answers and rate them as follows. Give yourself
One point for each questions that you answered "a", two
points for each "b" answer and three points for each "c"
answer. Add up your total score.

1-11) You are an inspiration to us. Keep it up!
12-20) Clutter, seems to be slowing you down. Start cutting
down your clutter a little at a time. Try de-cluttering your
sock drawer, or if you feel brave clean out the back seat of
your car.

21-33) Too much clutter is making you feel discouraged,
disorganized and frustrated, not to mention it's costing you
time and money. You need to read through this book thor-
oughly and apply some of these ideas.

Home Is A Mirror Reflection Of You
By Barry Birnberg
Interior Designer, Clairvoyant, Television Celebrity

Throughout the forty years of my work I have seen many client's homes and I get so much information about them, from their places, that they are often amazed when I reveal some of it back to them. It helps that I'm Clairvoyant. I wasn't always aware of that situation. I've learned to develop an insight, or to pick up clues, that even you can use to check out your own need for change.

A good example is a client's house I visited recently. I say house because immediately upon entering it, there was no feeling of a Home. My observation and investigative skills, lead me to understand that the house had never been altered to suit the owners and their family. In fact the house felt like a collection of distant relatives needing a family reunion.

Here are some of the clues that allowed me to feel the sense of a desperate house shouting out to be a Home.

Small dark paintings were displayed on the large entrance hall walls. There were no bright, "Joy of life", welcoming, pictures to be seen. A leftover dark brown cabinet faced the entrance door, holding an empty fish tank. Large multi-coloured vases were sitting on the cabinet including one that that was filled with grandiose dried or fake flowers. Very bad Feng Shui. Textured wallpaper dressed the wall behind the cabinet and worked its way out from the living room coming to a sudden stop as if it knew it didn't belong in the entrance. The wallpaper wasn't connected to any other walls in the entry foyer. Off the entrance

HOW DID WE GET SO CLUTTERED?

hall was a family room that had a piece of grey carpet hanging on one small wall. The same carpeting was, at one time, on the floor as well.

The dark grey/red tiled entrance floor seemed to represent the foreboding of what was to come. A dark, mahogany stained one foot high and four inches thick hand rail, connected with square antiqued bronze rails complete with grey carpeted stair treads opened from the basement up to the second floor. The side of the staircase wall leading to the basement was missing a four foot diameter (piece) area of paint. When one leaned over the handrail one could clearly see small golf ball pockmarks on the wall surfaces. Obviously the basement had been used by the family as a test location for their golf game.

The basement was also the place where all the past was dumped, but kept alive. There were four huge rooms in the basement that was once occupied by the daughter to escape into her own place. Now the rooms were filled with clutter representing memories of the past.

I asked about considering altering certain parts of the house, in order to bring it together as a "family unit". The response I got was that all the original material was never changed. It had been left by the original owners from sixteen years before. Other than a little paint here and there, not much else had been changed.

The reason was soon revealed. One of their daughters had come down with a very debilitating bone disease, one week prior to moving into the house. She has since rallied and become the beautiful, Pride and Joy of the whole family but for some eight years she was transported about in a wheelchair. In the sixteen years of occupying the house *there had been no interest in changing it.*

Part of my job, was to present the costs required to do these changes. I presented these costs, starting with the least expensive, painting exterior and interior and de-cluttering but they were not ready to undertake the measures.

Another fact was revealed, adding another dimension to the redesign of the "house to home" issue.
Both partners were in conflict as to whether to put out the funds to make it livable or to sell it. He wanted to sell while she was attached to all the negative memories.(that the house had entertained). The house was a negative reminder that all through the years she was the one responsible for being home caring for the child.

Was it worthwhile to do all the work at these costs? The final decision was made to fix it up, just cosmetically, in order to sell it. Once the work was done it was so pretty that the female partner found yet another reason to become attached. She wanted to hold onto the large, soon to be empty, 12 room home. Once again there was a conflict and they couldn't come to a decision about selling it.

I had to ask them both to sit quietly and visualize the home the way it would be if they stayed. The kids were now grown into adults and ready to move out on their own. There would be no sound of children to fill the house. There would be nothing but quiet, empty, unused spaces.

My strong feeling was that there was a need to have a place that sheltered, enveloped and warmly housed all that use it. A Home that fit who they are, not who they were. Perhaps by the time you read this I would have been given their decision. Email: b.birnberg@primus.ca

HOW DID WE GET SO CLUTTERED?

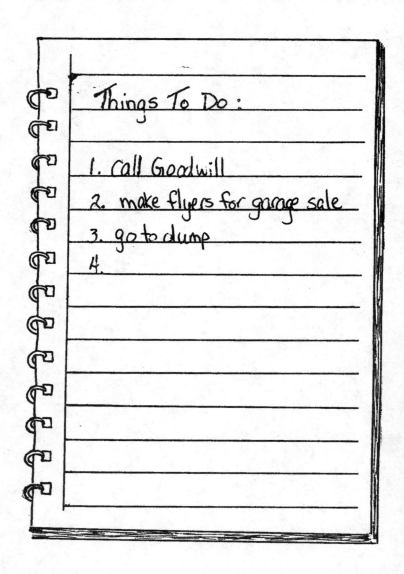

Chapter Three

Plan of Action

The goal is the thing

It is obvious by this point that you have made a decision to improve your life by removing the clutter. Question 1 of the Clutter Cutter Survey asked "What do you hope to learn from this workshop?" 25% answered that they were looking for some type of motivation. To get motivated or excited you need a reason or a goal. If you are not clear about where you are going, you end up standing still or going in circles. Having a goal gives you a clear picture of where you want to go.

Setting the time

In today's world it's not always easy to find TIME to do everything you want. Time is a valuable commodity so you should take a good look at how you are spending it. In the survey I asked the question, "Why do you think you have so much clutter?" 34.5% stated that it was because they had no time to clear it away. Obviously time is an issue for most people. In doing my research I came across something called a Time Log. The purpose of doing a time log is to itemize your daily activities. Since I was always stressed for time I decided to give the Time Log a try for myself. I kept track of my daily activities and after the first couple of days it was obvious to me that I was wasting much of my time on needless interruptions. After applying a few of the time saving tips I was able to free up at least 2-3 hours a day. If lack of time is holding you back read through the Time Management section in this chapter.

Unblocking the chi with Feng Shui
FENG SHUI, the art of placement is an excellent tool to help you locate and clear up stuff that is blocking your energy or chi. Feng Shui uses the natural laws of nature to determine the positive and negative flow of chi into a space. One of the key Feng Shui tools is the Pa Kua grid. This is an energy map that uses the compass to identify the eight areas of a space that relate to eight areas of your life. Once you've decided what your goals are you may want to check out the chi in your space. I have provided you with a brief look at Feng Shui and some of the basic principles you can use to help you focus in on areas of your space that need immediate attention. If things are not going well in your life maybe your chi is blocked.

GOAL SETTING
What are you making room for?

Why do you want to clear away your clutter? Do you want to feel at peace, be happy, find love, improve your life? You need to be much more specific about what you want or it will be difficult to achieve it. If you are not sure about what you want then try asking yourself a couple of simple questions. Ask what DON'T I want? Then ask, what DO I want? By eliminating what you don't want you are closer to what you do want. Most of the time the answers are not that simple. There is so much going on both in your head and in your surroundings and it becomes difficult to listen to your own thoughts. I suggest you find some quiet time, get up an hour earlier than normal or find a place where you can be alone with your thoughts. Let your own inner voice guide you. Tune in and let your own intuition guide you. Use some of the ideas below to help you realize some of your goals and desires.

Before you begin, take a few breaths and let your body and your mind relax. Focus on yourself for a change. Take a long sip of your coffee or herbal tea. Put on your comfy clothing and get relaxed. Have a pen and paper ready.

Flashback

Go into your memories as a small child. What did you love to do the most? What kind of games did you love to play? What did you love most about school? List some things that really motivated you. As a child what were your dreams? What did you want to become when you grew up? Did you achieve your goals or abandon them? What stopped you or what propelled you towards your goals? Think back and make a few notes.

Flash Forward

Look forward into the future. Advance forward five years from now. Where are you? What are you doing? Where are you living and with whom? What type of hobbies are you enjoying? Are you in the same career? Have you retired or changed jobs? When you are thinking about your future what are some of the challenges you think that you · may encounter? Write your thoughts down on paper.

The Goal Chart

After giving it some thought write down the things that feel right and make you happy. These ideas will help you develop a few goals for yourself. Your ideas may focus on your health, your family, your work or your home. Ask yourself exactly what and when you want these things..Take a look at the sample chart below and make up your own. The chart is just a guide to help you formulate a plan to follow. Tweak the plan as you go along. I suggest you write down the big goals or long-term future goals then fill in the smaller goals as you go along. In order for you to get to your ultimate goal you will need to take appropriate steps to get there. If it is a new home you are striving towards you will need to know how much it will cost and where it will be. Will this be possible in five years from now? Will you need to renovate your old home to increase it's value? Will you consider getting a better paying job? If you decide to get a new job will that require that you go back to school? Will you need a car?

Remember that these are your goals; not goals that others want for you. Keep updating and adding details. Goals should always be flexible and update as often as needed.

TIME	GOAL
1 Week	place ads in paper, have garage sale
1 Month	buy a computer, lose 5lbs
6 Months	finish basement, take writing course
1 Year	get full-time job
2 Years	pay off car, increase savings
5 Years	build new home, travel to Peru

The above chart is a sample of a personal goal sheet. Personal and business can be mixed or done separately. Once you have jotted down what your goals are you can go into more detail. For example if your immediate goal this week is to sell stuff in the paper or have a garage sale you can list who you need to call on your to-do list.

Write down your goal statement

Write down a clear statement of your dreams and goals. Use the present tense as if you have already attained it. Be specific and don't forget to include a time frame. One of your long-term goals may be to buy a home in the country and you would like to obtain this in five years. Shorter-term goals may be to write a book and complete it within the next three years. An immediate goal may be to clear out your office to make room for your research project for your upcoming book. Keep your statement where you can see it every day. Read it in the morning, afternoon and evening.

Meditate and Visualize

Meditate on a regular basis and visualize yourself achieving all of your goals.

Make a dream board

Dream boards create a visual picture to focus on. Clip out pictures, words or phrases from magazines and glue them onto a piece of paper or board. Your dream board is for your eyes only so anything goes. Place the dream board on a wall in your office or in your bedroom where you can see it everyday. A good idea is to make a smaller collage on a regular size sheet of paper, reduce it down and paste it directly on the inside of your date book or in your wallet.

TIME

I would, I could stand on a busy corner, hat in hand, and beg people to throw me all their wasted hours.
Bernard Berenson

The gift of time

If you received $1440 every day how would you use it? We are given this gift every day only it is 1440 minutes instead of dollars. There are 1,440 minutes in a day. How do you spend yours?

The time log

If you were asked to write down how you spent every minute yesterday could you do it? Below is an example of a Time or Activity Log. This tool is used extensively in both the corporate world as well as in universities and colleges. The purpose of it is to help you understand how you are spending your time and to help discover what times of the day that you are most productive. In this case a time log could be used to help you identify and remove all the time wasters that are cluttering up your day. It is suggested that you keep track of your time every day for a full week. The wonderful thing about this tool is that it is self-correcting. In other words you can see where there are problems and correct them the next day or next week. Take a sheet of paper with at least 20 lines on it and write down the following headings. See example below. Begin from the moment you wake up recording everything including sleeping and resting hours.

ACTIVITY	TIME	DURATION	PRIORITY	COMMENTS
Breakfast	8am	1 hour	A	too long
Banking	10am	45min	A	long line up
Phone calls	11am	20min	C	chatty sister
Watch TV	9pm	3 hrs	C	waste of time

Isn't it amazing how easy we forget how we spend our day? Perhaps there are things we don't want to remember or maybe we are so used to routine that we forget that it takes us 15 minutes to drive to the bank and that we had a coffee along the way and we stopped to talk to a neighbour on the way to the car. These few things alone may have accounted for some of the lost time.

After a few days of logging your time, analyze each activity. You may be alarmed to see the length of time you spend doing meaningless tasks and dealing with interruptions.

49

"We all have 24 hours in a day and 7 days in a week. And if you multiply that out and my math is correct (I assume it is because I've done this a few times), that gives us a total of 168 hours per week. And the thing about time is that it can only be spent, it cannot be saved. The average person is working in excess of 40 hours per week and I have found that most people lose about 3 hours per day or 15 hours per week in a Black Hole that sucks away and consumes better than a third of the quantity of time we have available to be productive in our work."The Hole Needless interruptions"
By: **Dr. Donald E. Wetmore**

The To-Do list

A to do list is a list of all the things you need to carry out each day. Generally you should only have ten items on the list, five personal and five business items. However if you are working on a large project you may want to break the project down to bite-size pieces and list the components on your to-do list. Keep your list in your spiral notebook rather than on loose sheets of paper. To-do lists are simple to use and can be one of the most valuable tools you use in keeping your day on track. Compile your to-do list first thing in the morning or the night before. To begin, list all of the tasks that need doing. Sort the tasks according to their importance, listing the most important thing first. Perhaps using a highlighter or coding them as A, B or C may work for you. Next batch the tasks into groups that can be done at the same time. If you find you have too many things to do in one day, try to delegate some of the tasks. See example below.

Sample To-Do List

1. Go to bank, deposit cheques   A
2. Pick up medication at drug store   A
3. Make business calls   A
4. Research info on current stock options   B
5. Make personal calls   C
6. Drop off clothes at Goodwill   C
7. Shop for new suit   C
8. Sort receipts for income tax return   C
9. Make dentist appointment   C
10. Meet Sally for coffee   C

Remember to list, prioritize and batch.

In the above list, number 1, 2 and 6 can be done at the same time. Number 9 should be done at the same time as 3 and 5. Combine 10 and 7. Number 8 should be priority A.

Date Books and Calendars

Some people love date books while others dislike using them. Having a date book is a good place in which to write your plans, plan your days and work your plans. Date books or day-timers can be simple or complicated; it's a matter of personal choice and need. One thing is for certain, having more than one date book can be complicated and clutter up your life. Both personal and business appointments should be kept in the same date book so that things don't overlap or get out of hand. Date books can be day-at-a-glance, weekly or month-at-a-glance. I personally prefer month-at-a-glance because in my line of work I book consultations and workshops months in advance. Some people plan detailed days while others work week by week. Stay away from Date books with pockets and separate compartments unless you are a very organized person. Complex multi-use date books tend to collect clutter and complicate things. There is a saying that goes; "some people spend too much time saddling up and not enough time riding".

Calendar Tips
◆Carry your date book with you at all times.
◆Record both business and personal dates.
◆Pencil in birthdays and anniversaries for the whole year.
◆Use your date book to record appointments and events and use your spiral notebook for other details and to-do lists.
◆Don't stash business cards and notes in your date book.
◆Schedule personal time or days off for yourself, and then work your appointments around your time off.

Responsibility Overload Syndrome
Is there not enough time in your day? Are you doing too much? Perhaps you are suffering from responsibility overload. Stress is often caused by trying to do too much. Even children today are being stressed out by too much extracurricular activity. I know this one woman with a 6 year old whose schedule is busier than mine. She is constantly driving him from one activity to another. As well as driving her son around she is on the PTA, Neighbourhood Watch Committee, President of the Newcomers Club and volunteers just about every time she is asked. Does this sound familiar? When a schedule is this full does this leave enough family and personal time? Many people report that they take on responsibilities because they don't like to dis-

appoint others as well as they don't want to be perceived as lazy.

Time is a very valuable commodity and how you spend it is up to you. No one should pressure you into giving them your time and make you feel guilty if you don't. There are many tools available to you to help you manage how you use your time. Remember that time cannot be managed but you can control how you spend it. Below are some tips on how you regain control and reduce your stressful schedule.

Time Tips
♦Learn how to say NO.
♦Select only one or two extra curricular activities for your children per season.
♦Volunteer your time only after you have scheduled time for yourself and family.
♦Call family and friends early in the morning and let them know that you will be busy and unavailable all day.
♦Utilize your answering machine or voice mail when busy.
♦Turn off your ringer when you're busy doing tasks.
♦Batch tasks together.
♦Reward yourself often.
♦Ask people to call before they come over to see you.
♦Read articles in your reading file while waiting for appointments or during down times.
♦Shop during down times. Try the 24-hour stores.
♦Bank on the phone or online or use the bank machine.
♦Get up an hour earlier every morning.
♦Delegate when possible.
♦Cook meals in large portions and freeze in small portions.

♦Always have a plan B rather than stressing over plan A
♦Do not give others permission to distract you
♦Work or play close to home when you have the option
♦Put a dollar value on your time and before you say yes calculate what it will actually cost

FENG SHUI
What is Feng Shui
Feng Shui is an ancient Chinese system of creating balance in your environment. More than 5,000 years old, it has now come of age. Introduced to the West about 100 years ago the basic principals of Feng Shui are as relevant today as they were then. Based on the five elements, the cycles of nature and the flow of energy, Feng Shui can be seen as an all-embracing view of the universe connecting heaven, earth and man. The scientific world acknowledges that the physical universe is not composed of matter but that its basic component is a kind of force or essence that we call energy. Although things may appear to be solid and separate from each other, on atomic and subatomic levels seemingly solid matter is seen as smaller and smaller particles. These fundamental particles are eventually reduced to just pure energy.

Physically, we are energy and everything around us is made up of energy. We are all part of one great energy field. Every molecule and atom, around and within us, vibrates at different rates of speed and has its own frequency and wavelength. Energy of certain quality or vibration tends to attract energy of a similar quality and vibration. All forms of energy are interrelated and can affect one another. All

PLAN OF ACTION

energy has both a positive and negative aspect. In Feng
Shui this is seen as polarities of yin and yang. The interaction between moving electrical charges and magnetic fields
is the underlying concept of Feng Shui. It shows us how to
tune in to the energies around us so that we can live in harmony with our surroundings. Feng Shui can influence and
help change life situations such as your career, health,
wealth, relationships and family life. It allows you to acti-
vate the powerful energies of the natural environment to
work in your favour and guide you to successful living.

Chi

Chi is the essence that is present in every element of the
cosmos. It is the life force energy that propels everything
into motion. Chi manifests itself in the atmosphere through
gentle breezes or powerful winds, and on the earth through
land formations such as mountains, hills and valleys. This
vital power is inhaled and exhaled, it expands and condens-
es, it is mass or it can be vapor. When Chi enters the depths
of the earth and expands, it can erupt as an active volcano,
which is similar to a person consuming contaminated food
and vomiting. In order for people to be healthy and prosperous the chi must be balanced and flow freely.

The Chinese have utilized the principles of chi for thousands of years. Martial artists demonstrate the power of chi
via the powerful strike of a single hand movement.
Acupuncturist use needles to tap into the body's meridian's
to unblock and balance chi. If chi could be observed by the
naked eye it would look like water moving in a stream or
river. The ideal condition would be for the water to be gen-

55

tly meandering. Large rocks and excess debris in the water interrupt the flow and force erratic conditions. A straight path would cause the water to move quickly and rapidly to it's destination. Water that is stuck in one spot with nowhere to go would eventually become stale and stagnate, creating a lifeless and noxious condition known as Sha Chi. Recognizing and utilizing the positive flow of chi in an environment is a vital component of Feng Shui.

Maintenance

Dead plants and dried flowers in the home and overgrown bushes and weeds give the impression of abandonment and neglect. Cracked driveways, walkways and windows catch Sha Chi between the cracks creating a sense of old age and staleness. A leaky faucet could mean your wealth is going down the drain. Broken appliances, objects and furniture attract negative energy and should either be fixed, recycled or thrown out.

Clutter

Everything is attached to you with a constantly tugging string. Clutter is one of the main causes of stale energy in and around the home. When chi enters your home it can get stuck in crowded corners, overstuffed closets, over-filled drawers or on messy counter tops. A good rule to follow is if you don't like it, don't need it or haven't used it in two years, get rid of it. Clearing clutter is one of the first and most important steps in practicing successful Feng Shui.

Blocks

In Feng Shui a block is that which stops or interrupts the

flow of chi, if a tree or branch fell across your driveway then its removal would be necessary. Overgrown trees blocking the view from a window or masking the entrance to your home are examples of blocks. Inside your home, excessive or oversized furniture and clutter in a small room can impede the flow of chi.

The Pa Kua

The Pa Kua is an octagon shaped tool that is used by Feng

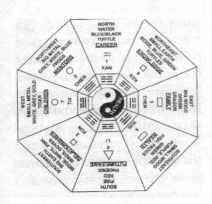

Shui practitioners to read energy within a space. Pa means eight and Kua means trigram and is taken from the ancient text of the I Ching. The Pa Kua is placed over the layout of a building, office, home, room or property and is used to locate areas of a space that relate to the eight areas of life The grid serves as a great tool to help you get motivated when clearing clutter. Review the list below and focus on the area of your life you would like to improve. Next, orient the Pa Kua over your space using compass direction. Observe what is occupying the space relating to those areas of your life that need work. Remove items that have no meaning and keep you in the past. Use the diagrams as a guide to help you identify clutter blocks that are blocking your chi.

Career - North

If trying to advance in a career this area should be clear of clutter and activated by adding water features such as fountains or fish tanks. Motivating pictures, diploma's or certificates should be placed on North walls.

Future -South

This sector represents your future goals and dreams. If your future is unclear you may have excess clutter blocking your future. Inspirational items and objects such as trophies, ribbons, awards, or travel pictures should be placed in this area.

Mentors-Northwest

The Northwest Kua represents Mentors and Spiritual help. Be sure that there is no undesirable symbolism or broken items or objects in the area. This is the best area to display statues or pictures of saints, angels, Buddha or anything that is spiritual in nature for you.

Children-West

This section corresponds to children, creativity and special projects. Display photographs of children, artwork and playful objects. This sector is good for a child's room, nursery or an art studio.

Personal Relationships-Southwest

This area relates to your significant other such as a spouse, lover or partner. If a meaningful relationship is what you are looking for, be sure you remove pictures, items and objects that are from past relationships. Also be sure there are no dead or dried flowers. Statues, clay pots and other earth objects should be placed in this area. Relationships can be enhanced and encouraged by putting things in pairs.

Knowledge-Northeast
The Northeast represents knowledge and wisdom so if you feel that you are not learning and growing, clear out this area. Get rid of old books, magazines, newspapers or any items that have no meaning. Frame inspirational poems or sayings and place them on the wall in this section.

Family-East
This area represents family, ancestors, community and friends. These are people who have great influence in your life. Family portraits, heirlooms, keepsake, and memorabilia should be kept in this area. Too much stuff can result in stagnant or turbulent relationships. This sector influences health so keep it well maintained and free from clutter.

Wealth-Southeast
This area corresponds to money, prosperity and self-enpowerment. Keep this area well lit, clear of clutter and place healthy plants, red candles or a tabletop fountain in this area if appropriate for the room.

Pa Kua Mapping (based on compass direction)
Begin by drawing a sketch of your living space. You can work with the main floor of your home or you can work on

an individual room.

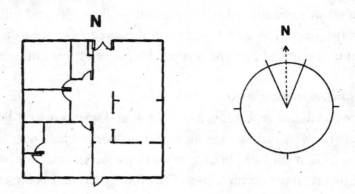

Find the center of the space and determine compass directions. The compass indicator will usually point North.

Place the Pa Kua Grid over the space by first matching the center of the Pa Kua Grid with the Centre of the room.

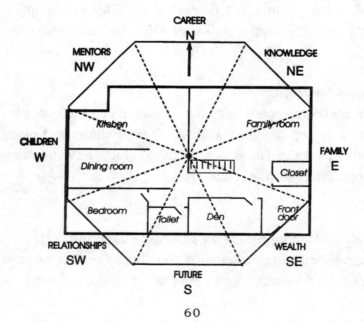

Next Turn the grid so that the arrow in the center of the North Sector is lined up with the compass North.

Tip

Make a clear copy of the Pa Kua Grid and then place it over your space so that you can see exactly where each of the areas are located in your space.

For more information on Feng Shui read Seven Step Feng Shui by Lina Visconti. (listed in recommended reading section in back of book).

CLUTTER CUTTER GUIDE

Discover Your Inner Voice

By Joshua M. Zuchter, B.A.
Empowerment Specialist

A friend and I were discussing names that he and his wife were coming up with to name their baby when it was born. I playfully said, "Tom, I'm picking up on a name if it's a boy. You could name him Joshua. It just came to me, so it must be true".
And then he and I proceeded to laugh as we were both aware that this experience was not a so-called intuition for the most appropriate name for his baby. Rather, it was an awareness of what my mind was thinking and served as a message regarding how important the name is to me. How often do you hear of others saying they think they know what's best for someone else, possibly by using their intuition, when perhaps the information was likely best for themselves, from the chatter of their mind?

Intuition is natural, creative, fluid, and miraculous. Although it occurs at very subtle levels of consciousness, everyone can choose to tune in tu it. The greatest challenge often lies in discerning between intuition and the chatter (in Feng Shui we call it clutter).

There are four ways of experiencing intuition: as a vision, as an auditory sound/phrase, as a feeling, and as a knowing. Regardless of which one you experience, realize that these intuitions come without having to put any effort into them. The only effort that is required is in the listening, looking, feeling, and sensing for them with an inner awareness.

Some of the most popular movies that have been out in theaters display notions of intuition. For example: "Feel the force...", and "My Spidey sense is tingling."

Many of us are fortunate in that when we are tuned in we have visions. This is different from a visualization that may take several minutes, in which you picture what you may do tomorrow morning upon awakening. In a vision, you would see the big picture, including what you will do tomorrow morning, afternoon, and evening. Furthermore, it will take less than a second to see it all.

Another type of intuition is a knowing, which is prophetic in nature. Have you ever known something that you couldn't explain how you knew, you just did? Different from knowing something that is taught to you and therefore learned, a prophetic knowing lacks any reasoning to explain how you know the particular information that you know. Have you heard others use the excuse, "I just know"? It's as if it were written in their minds even before they were born.

A feeling, usually also called a sense, is another type of intuition. You either feel and have a good sense or feel bad and have a heavy nagging sense. This type of intuition is one that most people are aware of, as many can relate to "gut instincts" or "going with their hearts".

Lastly, but certainly not least, is an auditory intuition. If you read this paragraph out loud, listen to yourself reading it. Then, quiet down slowly until you are reading it to yourself silently and continue to listen. An auditory intuition is very similar, yet much more subtle. I remember driving along a highway several years back. It was a beautiful day. The sky was pure blue with just a few fluffy clouds. There were barely any cars on the road so I felt as if I was the only one on the highway. It was during autumn and therefore cool, but I was quite comfortable. I was focused, relaxed, centered, and peaceful... some would say I was "present". And all of the sudden, I heard a quote as if someone were saying it aloud to me... "Responsibility is the amount of growth one chooses to accept"... That was a very profound experience for me... Was I tuning in to intuition?... I think so. I had never read that quote or heard of it before that time... and the radio was off. I realized from that experience how powerful intuition, and hence presence, truly are. As the mind experiences stillness, presence is the outcome. When we are focused, relaxed, and aware in that state of stillness, we are able to slip into the space between thoughts, where infinite wisdom exists.

Quantum physicists and some philosophers propose that all things consist of energy and are connected in a type of matrix or web that links all matter in some way. In Chinese tradition this may be represented by the term Chi, which is often referred to in Feng Shui.

Is it possible that an intuition is simply a tuning into the web or energy of life that allows us to experience insights such as $E=mc2$ or other prophetic knowings?

Perhaps the only way to know this is by tuning in. To be able to see, know, feel, and hear intuitions, presence is key. A powerful technique for pursuing 'being in the moment' is meditation. You may find the following simple technique allows you to tune in to that web, the universe, higher self, or matrix that exists in the space between your thoughts.

Exercise:

1. Go out into a park or somewhere that you feel safe, peaceful, and comfortable that is free from distractions.

63

2. Sit or lie down, close your eyes and be aware of your breath. As you breathe in through your nose be aware of how you feel as air enters your body and fills your diaphragm. Be aware of how you feel as you exhale through your nose. Feel your diaphragm contract as air exits your lungs. Continue to do this for a couple of minutes.

3. With your eyes still closed be aware of what you hear, smell, taste, and feel with your senses from the outside in. At that point, if you are dealing with a challenge in your life, ask a specific question as to how to deal with that challenge or ask to achieve or experience clarity with it. Be aware of images, visions, feelings, knowings or sounds that come to you from the inside out... Spend some time in this moment, being aware of what is coming to you. Simply allow pictures, feelings, sensations, and/or phrases to come. Spend a few moments in this experience.

4. When you are ready, bring your awareness back to how you feel, the wind brushing your cheek, gravity pulling you down comfortably to the earth, and slowly open your eyes. Begin to move around slowly and easily.

This is a particularly useful technique that you can use to spend some quality time with yourself at least once a day for 30 minutes. As you honor yourself more and more, your ability to discern between the clutter of the mind and intuition (visions, sounds and phrases, feelings, and knowings) will grow.

In sum, we all have a natural ability within us to see, know, feel, and hear our true selves, to connect with our Beingness and everything that we truly desire in all aspects of our lives. Wayne Dyer put it best when he said, "Prayer is you talking to God. Intuition is God talking back."

When you clear the clutter of your mind, your ability to see, hear, feel, and know will expand and it is then that you will be more able to tap into the matrix of life that we call Being.

Joshua is a graduate of the University of Western Ontario where he studied Psychology. With an interest in the field of communications and human interaction Josh also has a background in the ancient healing modalities of Reiki and Qi Gong, and has studied various martial arts as well as Feng Shui more recently. Please contact him for more information about his keynotes, playshops, and public seminars. He can be reached at 519-657-8630 or e-mail: joshua@symmetria.com

Chapter Four

Space Clutter

This chapter relates to any thing that takes up space other than paper . Paper clutter is featured in chapter five. Read through this chapter before you decide to de-clutter. Begin by filling in the Clutter Location Chart below so that you have a clear sense of which project you should begin with. Whether you decide to de-clutter your wardrobe, organize your photos or go through your kid's toys there are plenty of tips and time saving ideas in this chapter. If you decide to work on an entire room refer to the Room by Room de-clutter tips. Whatever project you choose to work on first be sure you schedule enough time for it. For example if you are cleaning a garage you will need a full day but if you just want to clean out your bathroom set aside a few hours. Use the clutter location chart below as a guideline to help you determine where to begin. As you are filling in the chart be sure to rate it as a priority A, B or C. You can work on the C priorities anytime but the A priority list should be done first.

CLUTTER LOCATION CHART				
LOCATION room	CLUTTER *stuff/paper*	SPECIFY *items*	PRIORITIZE *A,B,C*	SCHEDULE *days/hours*
Attic				
Bedroom				
Bathroom				
Basement				
Car				
Dining Room				
Family Room				
Deck/Balcony				
Garage				
Hallway				
Hobby Room				
Kitchen				
Laundry				
Office				

FIVE BOX SORTING SYSTEM

I believe that the Five Box system is an excellent way to begin the clutter cutting process. This method helps break down the job into manageable pieces and is less intimidating. When the space is too small for boxes simply place things in piles on the floor.

Materials
♦Five or more cardboard boxes that have a lid and handles on the side.
♦Notebook and a pen
♦Masking tape
♦Cleaning Supplies

Label each box as follows; Garbage, Gift/Donate, Relocate/Store/Put Away, Fix/Clean/Finish, and Holding Tank. These are just suggested names for items as outlined in the following descriptions. You may want make up your own names or add a box or two as you go along. The important thing is that you put things in like categories. The best way to start is by throwing things into the Garbage box since this will be the easiest and most obvious stuff to get rid of. Read through the five category descriptions and then follow Clutter Cutter - Step by Step

Garbage
Line this box with a garbage bag so that the box can easily be reused. This is for obvious garbage such as candy wrappers, broken items, and anything else that has no purpose for you. Remember that if it is garbage for you no one else should have it either.

Gift/Donate
This box is for things that you don't have use for but are too good to throw away. You keep packing, stashing, dusting, moving it around and keeping it, just in case you may need it. Gifting is a wonderful way to get rid of clutter. There is no better feeling than seeing your stuff being put to use by

someone else. Consider donating to the Salvation Army, Goodwill, women's shelters, halfway homes, churches, hospitals, schools and libraries.

Relocate
The relocate box is for items and objects that don't belong in the area you are working in. Mugs and plates don't belong on your desk. A tennis racquet does not belong in your bedroom closet. You may find a Cross pen that belongs to someone else in which case you should made a note on your list to give this person a call. This is also the box for things you've borrowed and have been meaning to return.

Fix
This box is for clothing with missing buttons, broken picture frames, unfinished crafts and stained or soiled items or objects that are cleanable. Note that if any of these items are beyond repair they should be tossed into the garbage box. If you haven't touched that hobby yarn for 5 years, you probably won't. Consider putting it in the Gift box. This box requires action so if you really don't think it's worth fixing and keeping or fixing and giving away put in the GARBAGE BOX.

Hold
This box is for items and objects that you can't make a decision on. Rather than stressing over them just place them in this box and make a decision later. WARNING: This box represents indecision - if the box gets too full there is a message here for you. Once this box is filled date it. Don't

worry you can take another look in it later.

Cut the Clutter -Step by Step

1. Review your long and short term goal statement and take a look at the Feng Shui Pa Kua Grid and locate areas of your space that may need to be unclogged.

2. Schedule time for the task. Make a time commitment and write it down on your calendar.

3. On the day of the task call all your relatives, friends and let them know that you will be very busy all day and that you will not be taking any calls.

4. Gather your materials in a handy carrying basket.

5. Line up your five labeled boxes in front of you

6. Begin by taking everything out of every drawer, closet and cupboards. Look under and behind every piece of furniture and leave no stone unturned.

7. Pick up every item and make a decision about it. As you handle each item ask yourself the following questions:

Do I need this?

Do I love this?

Is this keeping me in the past?

What would happen if this were lost forever?

Does this support my goal?

Can someone else make better use of this?

Be sure to jot down reminders in your notebook for your to-do list. Calls should be scheduled for the next day or when time permits.

8. Once you have gone through every item and placed them in the appropriate boxes, keep things moving by taking the boxes out of the room and into the hall or garage. Take the Gift box items directly to your car for distribution and the Garbage to the curbside.

9. At this point you should do a secondary sorting with the Fix/Repair box and review step number 8. Remember to make notes as to what you plan on doing with the items.

10. Take a quick look in the Hold box and if you still can't make a decision then seal it, date it and store it away. Keep contents for a year and if you still haven't decided - Get rid of it.

11. Clean and vacuum the space you have just cleared.

12. Relocate items back into their proper place. Remember that everything you put back is put there by choice not by accident. If you are de-cluttering your office you should only have piles of paper left on the desk (refer to Paper Clutter in next chapter)

13. Take a mental picture of the space or take a photo to remind you of this moment.

14. You have now taken back control of your space. Time to sit back, relax and reward yourself.

Tips

♦If the job seems too big or overwhelming - GET HELP!!

♦Play your favourite music while you de-clutter. Of course you can always play the old time favourites "Please release me and let me go, cause I don't love you anymore", or how about "50 ways to loose your clutter, just toss it out the back, Jack, make a new plan, Stan, you don't need to be coy, Roy, just listen to me".

♦Schedule the right amount of time needed to complete job

SPACE CLUTTER - by Category

Some of the most common items that seem to accumulate

fall under the following categories; art, clothing, containers, collectables, memorabilia, ornaments, photos and toys.

Art
♦Do not display negative or depressing art in key areas
♦Rotate artwork according to season
♦Photocopy kids art, reduce and place in scrapbooks
♦Photocopy in colour, enlarge, frame and display kids' best artwork
♦Purchase magnetic frames to display artwork on fridge
♦Store kids artwork in plastic bins, there is no need to display everything

Clothing
♦ Hang tall/longer clothes in the back and short in the front.
♦Keep items off the floor
♦Buy coloured plastic hangers and colour code clothing. Blouses on white hangers and skirts on blue etc.
♦Hang skirts and pants on hangers with clips
♦Donate metal hangers to the cleaners or give away with clothing
♦If you don't like it or it does not fit, give it away
♦Keep clothing with colours that suit you***
♦Consider selling expensive clothing in high end consignment shops
♦Locate a good seamstress in your area to do alterations
♦ Give outdated clothing to charity or local theatre groups
♦If on a diet, keep only a few items for measure only. Purchase new clothing once you reach and keep your desired weight
♦For every item you purchase get rid of one item (one in

and one out)

♦Repair or toss out damaged, stained, worn, or faded clothing and shoes.

♦Keep clothing clean and pressed and ready to wear

♦Rotate clothing in your closet according to season

♦Place sport clothing/workout wear and costumes in a separate closet

♦Toss out single socks or gloves

♦Give away any clothing that does not support your current goals

♦Toss out or give away clothing with negative association

♦Review your accessories and toss out items not worn in the last year. *Give away costume jewelry that doesn't match your goals or wardrobe

♦Have a colour consultant do your colours. Did you know that some colours make you look drab and sick while others make you look healthy and exciting! This is one of the most worthwhile de-clutter tips you will get. Once you know your true colours you can sort, match and choose only the items that will suit you.

Containers

♦Use an empty Kleenex box to hold plastic bags (1 box holds 50 bays)

♦Use leftover wallpaper to decorate empty coffee cans, diaper wipe boxes and shoeboxes and use them to store small like items such as buttons and beads

♦Small jars can be used to store items such as paper clips, nut, bolts, nails and spices

♦Cardboard boxes are great for storing Christmas items and lighter items

♦Break down large cardboard boxes and store flat in garage or basement

♦Use plastic see-through containers to store clothing, toys and crafts

♦Get rid of plastic containers that have missing lids or purchase fitted plastic covers (available in grocery stores - they look like shower caps)

♦Resist the urge to collect margarine bins or set a limit

♦ Use jars to store rice, pasta, spices and other dried foods

♦Small audio tape containers are great for displaying business cards, just open and invert to form a self standing card holder (excellent for networking meetings)

♦Donate egg cartons to nursery schools and preschools for making crafts

♦Recycle baskets and use for gift giving

♦Keep markers and labels handy to identify contents of containers

♦Keep container sizes consistent for easy storage

Memorabilia

♦Keep memorabilia such as ticket stubs, programs and newspaper clippings in a scrapbook (one scrapbook per family member)

♦ Photocopy and reduce items and place on a single page

♦Make quilts or wall hangings from favourite/sentimental clothing

♦Take a picture of larger memory items, give away, file, frame or display the photo

♦Keep similar items together such as all ribbons, trophies

♦Photograph, frame and display pictures of fresh flowers,

instead of keeping dried flowers

♦Purchase a pretty memory box for letters and small items you cherish

Ornaments

♦Clear space by removing and storing away half your ornaments. Rotate your ornaments and group, keeping like objects together

♦Remove any negative or depressing objects from key areas

♦ Refrain from buying souvenirs on your next vacation

♦Fix or toss out any broken or chipped objects

Photos

♦Arrange photos by time frame or event

♦Give away your doubles or toss them out

♦Throw out photos that cut peoples' heads off or that have thumbprints on them.

♦Get rid of photos of people, places and objects that have no meaning.

♦Make theme collages, frame and hang on your walls

♦Give collages of pictures, as gifts to your friends, children and family.

♦Place multiple photos together on one sheet, copy and reduce.

♦Arrange photos on tables, end tables and desks and cover with glass.

♦Pick out the best of pictures and get rid of the rest

♦Purchase photo albums and photo boxes that are the same size for easy storage.

♦Have photos put on photo CD, slides or use a digital camera with micro disc

♦When framing large or small photos be sure to group by theme

♦Photographers take dozens of similar shots and only keep the best ones

Toys

♦Use see-through plastic tubs with lids to store toys
♦Label toys as indoor, outdoor, upstairs or downstairs
♦Small decorative boxes work well for Barbie clothing and accessories.
♦Use space under beds and bottom of closets to store boxes
♦Cover a pole, post or rod with material; attach velcro and use for storing stuffed animals .
♦Purchase a crate, trunk or bench with storage space for bulky toys.
♦Decorate, and or, colour code plastic containers for easy recognition of contents.

SPACE CLUTTER TIPS - Room by Room
Bathroom

♦Keep reading material at a minimum. Health magazines are best.
♦Go through cleaning products and keep necessary items in one basket or carrying case
♦Empty out the medicine cabinet. Dispose of expired and unused medication on your next trip to the pharmacy.
♦Keep prescriptions in a dark, dry area. A high kitchen cupboard is best; washrooms are damp.
♦Gift away any small sample sizes of soap, shampoo and creams.
♦Keep extra supplies of toilet paper, shampoo and other

products packed away in the hall closet.

♦Toss out makeup that is more than 6 months old.

♦Dispose of any toxic products that have been sitting around.

♦Try to use non-toxic natural products when possible.

♦Use baking soda as an all-purpose cleaner.

♦Toss out old potpourri and replace with scented candles.

♦Gift away any gadgets that you don't use or need.

Bedroom

♦Bedrooms are personal places and should be kept as clear as possible.

♦Invest in a storage trunk if space is limited.

♦Purchase large plastic containers to store seasonal clothing and shoes.

♦Use the space under your bed to store large plastic containers.

♦Utilize the inside of your door to hang shoe caddy, tie or scarf rack.

♦Use a decorative box to store candles and aromatherapy oils.

♦Keep dirty clothing in a closet hamper.

♦Limit the amount of magazines and books in the bedroom.

♦De-clutter wardrobes each season and gift away what you don't use.

Garage and Tool Sheds

♦Utilize the walls and store smaller boxes on shelves and sports equipment on pegs.

♦Remove and throw away any rusted or broken items.

♦Utilize half-full containers of paint for garage walls or tool sheds.

♦Measure out a large piece of wood, trace your tools, affix nails or pegs and hang tools up.

♦Instead of having many tools consider getting all-in-one tools and gift away what you don't need.

♦Flatten down cardboard boxes and put together when needed.

♦Use small jars for nails, nut, bolts and small items.

♦ Donate your old car to your local mechanic school.

Kitchen

♦Toss out chipped or broken plates, cups and glasses.

♦Gift away extra sets of dishes, pots and utensils.

♦Divide junk drawers into plastic, wood and metal.

♦Keep dry food in plastic containers and do away with bulky boxes.

♦Put spices in glass jars, label and keep together .

♦Place a notebook with a pen attached near the telephone for messages.

♦Keep operating manuals and warranties together in a box.

♦Give away unused, unwanted tins and boxes of food to the Food Bank.

♦Toss out plastic containers that have no lids.

♦Keep labels and pens handy for making ID stickers.

Office

♦Cut down on paperwork by having only one calendar for both personal and business.

♦Use spiral notebook for phone calls, to-do-list and reminders

♦Have only two drawers when filing paperwork, active and

permanent.

♦Use simple, easy-to-use file systems rather than complex ones.

♦Keep a paper shredder under your desk.

♦Remove ornaments and knickknacks from desks.

♦Toss out envelopes as soon as you remove contents.

♦Mail back advertising inserts with bill payments.

♦Gift away computers and outdated equipment to charities.

♦Use tray divider on desk for paperclips, white out and stapler.

♦When buying new furniture or equipment ask if they can recycle your old stuff.

♦Keep stuff off floors and utilize the vertical space on the wall.

♦Reduce books on bookcase by only keeping what you use regularly.

♦Use a vertical CD holder that can be mounted on walls.

Now that you have cleared away your clutter keep it moving, right out the door. You should have several boxes full of stuff to throw out, recycle, give away or sell. Go through your holding box to see if you can reduce the amount of stuff in that box. Next go to the fix and repair box and ask yourself if you really intend on fixing or repairing these things. Before disposing of unwanted stuff and garbage read through the Resources section as well as Chapter Six which deals with Environmental Clutter.

Chapter Five

Paper Clutter

Do you remember when they said that the computer would help us move towards a paperless society? That was the biggest fib that was ever told. The truth is, we have paper filling our landfill now more than ever. Office paper tops the list, followed by books, magazines and publications. The problem is, we are producing paper clutter faster than our landfill can break it down. Obviously cutting down on your consumption of paper is first order of the day, however first you need to get out from under the piles of paper you have buried yourself in.

What is Paper Clutter?
Below, is an alphabetical list of many of the common paper clutter groups. Without looking around, check off items that

clutter your home and desk. You'll see them in your mind's eye because these things clutter up your head as well. Later in this chapter I have provided tips for the most common items that seem to pile up.

❏ Bank Statements
❏ Books
❏ Boxes
❏ Bill Statements/Invoices
❏ Business Cards
❏ Catalogues
❏ Certificates
❏ Computer Printouts
❏ Coupons
❏ Credit Card Statements
❏ File Folders
❏ Flyers
❏ Gift Wrap
❏ Greeting Cards
❏ Junk Mail
❏ Kid's Artwork

❏ Kid's Reports
❏ Letters
❏ Legal Papers
❏ Magazines
❏ Mail
❏ Maps
❏ Newspapers
❏ Note Paper
❏ Operating Manuals
❏ Old School Papers
❏ Phone Books
❏ Photographs
❏ Receipts
❏ Recipes
❏ Tax Returns
❏ Travel Brochures
❏ Warranties

Cutting down paper clutter can be a huge undertaking however if you break things down into smaller tasks they are less intimidating. Decide to tackle one task at a time and be sure that you schedule enough time to complete the job. Begin by working on one of the common categories such as photographs or artwork. You may find the tips and suggestions to be immediately gratifying. Whatever project you decide to work on, be sure to have the proper materials on hand.

Supplies
Scissors, exacto knife, paper shredder (or a box labeled, "to be shredded"), garbage bags, recycling boxes, all-purpose three-ring notebook, five general sorting boxes or containers, stapler, cleaning solution and cloth, vacuum cleaner, scotch tape, masking tape, bottled water, pens, highlighter, black magic marker and motivating music.

General Sorting - step by step
1. Review your goal.
2. Use the Five Box System (chapter four) for basic sorting. If your space is too small for boxes put things in piles on floor or in hallway.
3. As you handle each item make a decision on it. Place each item into appropriate box or pile.
4. Open every drawer, cupboard, envelope and file cabinet until completely empty.
5. Clean, dust and vacuum before you return items to their proper place.
6. Keep all loose paper to one side for the moment.
7. Clear everything off desk and place items in a box labeled "desk items"
8. Use the clear desk surface to sort paper. If working from your kitchen or living room use a table or flat surface.

At this point you should have a pile of papers sitting on your desk or table, that may include letters, bills, documents and correspondence. You should feel like you are beginning to gain back control, because all the paper that was scattered about is now sitting in one place. You are now ready to begin sorting through the paper clutter that has been creating chaos in your space.

LOOSE PAPER

To sort out your loose paperwork use this simple system that I refer to as FRAGS. You can use little trays, boxes or just place the papers in categories using the headings File, Refer, Act, Garbage and Stop. I use the acronym F.R.A.G.S.

F.R.A.G.S. Sorting System
File

This section is for your FILE PILE. There are things you are required to keep: income tax returns, medical records etc. For ideas on file systems refer to the suggestions later in this chapter.

Refer

This category is for papers, letters and notes that can be passed on and handled by someone else. Use File Folders to direct papers to the appropriate people.

Act

Never pick up a piece of paper and not act on it. If the paper requires you to answer it right away, do it. It may be a good idea to keep an action tray on your desk. Obviously, if it is 2am you may want to wait for the next day .

Garbage

This is for obvious garbage such as candy wrappers and

used tissues. Papers that are considered garbage can be shredded or put into a recycle box. For more on recycling refer to Environmental Clutter (chapter six)

Stop
This is for newsletter subscriptions, junk mail, mailing lists and advertising bulletins. Review each item, then ask yourself if this is supporting your current goals. This is one of the biggest paper challenges. One of the most effective ways of keeping paper from piling up is to STOP it before it comes through the door. Take a marker and write the word "Cancel" on subscriptions. Write down phone numbers and make a decision to have yourself removed from mailing lists. If time permits make the call right away or leave until the next day. A good idea is to keep a recycling box by the front door for junk mail.

At this point you are ready for secondary sorting. The first and easiest pile to get rid of is the garbage. Take the pile to the garage or curbside. The Refer, Act and Stop piles are considered action files and should be worked on during the appropriate hours. However the File pile should be addressed as soon as possible. If you don't have a file system consider some of the suggestions below. Use these suggestions as guidelines for setting up your own unique system.

FILE SYSTEMS
There are three categories for filing paperwork, Active, Reference and Archives. The samples below can be used for either Personal or Professional or a combined filing system.

There is no right or wrong way to file, what's important is that it's easy for you to find your paperwork.

ACTIVE

These are your active or working files. You may work on them once a week, once a month or daily. Either way it is best to keep them where you can access them when needed.

Don't ask yourself where can I file it, ask yourself where can I find it if when I need it.

REFERENCE

Once you have completed working on a file or a piece of paper you may want to put it in your permanent reference file. These files can get pretty thick so be ruthless when you file in your permanent file.

Did you know that 80% of all papers filed are never looked at again?

ARCHIVES

Purge your reference file on a regular basic and if you feel you still may need to refer to them place them in your archives and keep and file by the year. Archive files should be kept in boxes and out of the way like in the garage or basement.

Did you know that executives waste over 100 hours per year looking for documents and that only 1 in 20 documents are lost and are never found.

You may choose to file monthly, numerically or alphabetically. Any of these systems can be used for either personal or business files. Choose a simple file system that works best for you. Below are samples of systems that are easy to use.

MONTHLY Filing System
Used for Active Files
34 Hanging Files
31 folders for each day of the month
1 in the front for Current Paperwork
2 in the back for Next Month and Next Year
or
45 Hanging Files
31 folders for each day of the month
12 for each month of the year
1 for next year
1 pending

This system can be used for paying invoices and bills. When a bill is received, write out the cheque right away, put it into an envelope, affix stamp and file under the day that it is to be mailed. Check in "today's folder" each day and complete the tasks at hand. Once the file is empty move it into the next month. If paperwork does not need to be addressed until next month or next year, place it in the proper hanging folder and deal with it at that time.

NUMERICAL Filing System
Use for Active or Reference Files
Numbers are easy to recognize at a glance. This system is especially good if you have many reference files. Use

hanging file folders just like in the first drawer only you will be numbering each file in order i.e. 1, 2, 3, 4, 5, 6, 7, 8 and so on. You can keep numbering as many as you need. Have a marker and file folder next to your papers that you need to file. Begin to sort through your file pile one paper at a time. Decide what categories you would like to use as you glance at each paper. For example you may come across an advertisement for window tinting in which case you may want to call this AUTO stuff. Take that sheet of paper and put it into the #1 file labeled "AUTO". Go to the next sheet of paper and that may be some special notice about upcoming spas' special. Place that sheet in number #2 file and label it SPAS. Go through each paper until there is nothing left. Remember you may come across an item that relates to paper you have already filed so you may not need more than 20 categories. Below is a sample of what your filing may look like.

sample

FILE #	CONTENT
Write on top corner	Write in subject space
1	AUTO
2	SPAS
3	SOCCER
4	CHURCH
5	DENTIST
6	VETERINARY
7	BANK

Once you have filled all your files. Take a sheet of paper and write down what is in each file. Next arrange the files in order by number into the PERMANENT FILE drawer. Take your list and rearrange it so that you are putting the content side in alphabetical order. This sheet will become your master file and should be kept handy. It should look like this:

CONTENT	FILE #
AUTO	1
BANK	7
CHURCH	4
DENTIST	5
SOCCER	3
SPAS	2
VETERINARY	6

The files should be in your drawer and you should be left only with a sheet of paper listing the file contents. Any time you need a file, look it up alphabetically on your "MASTER LIST" and then simply open your PERMANENT FILE DRAWER and look up the file number. You may want to make sub-files. For example, if your AUTO file gets too thick you may want to create another file and call it 1A - AUTO-INSURANCE file.

ALPHABETICAL File System
Use for active, reference or archives
File by Main Category and then divide into sub categories. Below is a sample of how easy it is to categorize and then sub-categorize the alphabetical file system. This list will help you come up with headings that work best for you.

Personal File Sample

91

Auto, window tinting, Corolla, Tundra, detailing, repairs
Banking, savings, joint, personal
Beauty, spas, hair, skin, massage
Certificates, certification, completion, birth, marriage
Charity, CNIB, MADD, CCS
Church, Rummage Sale, Schedule, Rev. Jacob
Communications, cell, pager, palm pilot
Community, soccer team, neighbourhood watch, rotary club
Family, John, Mary, Rebecca, Robert
Health, Dr. Jane, Dentist, Herbal
Hobbies, Crafts, needlepoint, watercolour, pottery
Home Improvements, deck, garden, basement, garage
Investments, stocks, mutual funds
Inventory, bank accounts, safe, safety deposit box
Insurance, auto, home, personal
Legal, divorce papers, home deed, car ownership
Pets, Vet, Panda, Sonja, Jaxx
Receipts, gas, restaurant, cleaners, courses, travel expenses
Resumes, John, Mary
School, PTA, fundraisers
Sports, bike club, soccer, volleyball
Travel, Cruises, Safari
Utilities, telephone, hydro, gas, water, cable
Warranties and Guarantees, TV, DVD, VCR, dishwasher

Professional File Sample
Affiliations, union, BBB
Auto, lease, detailing, Matrix
Banking, business account, ING direct
Credit Card, business Visa
Customers, client list disk backup

Government, laws, rulings, incorporation
Certificates, speed reading, Feng Shui basics
Courses, power point, internet business
Receivable, mutual funds
Receivable, web hosting, email accounts
Landlord, JJ Smith and assoc., JR Holdings
Legal, leases, licenses
Office Equipment, computer, fax, storage systems
Payable, ETR, subscription
Payroll, casual help, secretary
Real Estate, Muskoka lot, cottage
Receipts, gas, travel
Receivable, contracts, invoices
Resume, profiles
Staff, resumes, background checks
Suppliers, retail, wholesalers, independent contractors
Tax, PST, GST, corporate
Telephone, cellular, pager, office line
Travel, CAA, Frequent Flyer Points, Air Miles

Alphabetical filing is best for storing closed files. Be sure to purge on a regular basis. Every business is different so check the industry standards for keeping files.

Archive Tips
♦File alphabetical or numerical as above
♦Use stackable boxes with lids and label with date and contents
♦Store the box in a separate location such as basement or garage and purge at least once a year.

Did you know that 80% of all papers filed are never read again?

COMMON PAPER CLUTTER *by Category*
Listed below are the most popular tips and suggestions for the different paper categories.

Bank Statements
♦Reconcile your cheques and wrap the statement around the cheques with an elastic. File in a box by the year.

Bills
♦Place all incoming bills in a separate tray or in your active file, filed by utility. Open a bill right away; write out the cheque put in envelope with stamp and place in ACTIVE file under the appropriate date.
♦Set up a bill payment center. Include your bill file, stamps, envelopes, return-address labels, checkbook and calculator. Put all items together in a portable basket so bills can be worked on in any location of your home.
♦Print label sheets for addresses frequently used. Quickly retrieve a label when you are ready to send outgoing mail.
♦Keep credit card receipts together until the bill arrives.
♦Verify items before paying the bill. Put receipt away or toss out.
♦Reduce your credit cards. Keep one for personal use and one for business use to simplify bill paying and the amount of incoming paperwork. Switch to low-interest and no annual fee credit cards.
♦Consider paying regular monthly bills by automatic deduction from your bank account or through on-line ser-

vices. Save time and save money on stamps and cheques.

Books

♦Put away, make a gift of, or donate books you no longer have use for, especially fiction paperbacks. Keep all reference books handy. Use the vertical space in the room to shelve books and group by category. Keep recipe books in the kitchen.

♦Give away all books that do not support your current goal in life.

Business Cards/Addresses

♦Put all your business cards in a recipe box and purge regularly. Use alphabetical file or file as you get them, filing the latest card in the front.

♦You can also use a decorative box to house all of your business cards along with envelopes and slips of paper with addresses.

♦Tear off addresses from envelopes or papers and staple on to a single sheet of paper. Photocopy the sheet or type into your database when you have time.

Catalogues and Phone Books

♦Store catalogues and phone books in a separate location from newspapers and magazines.

♦Categorize large numbers. Recycle as new ones arrive.

♦Remove your name from unwanted catalogue mailings. Cut off your name and address label and return it with a simple typed request for removal. Keep extra copies of note for future mailings.

Certificates

♦Frame certificates and display only those that support your current goal and file the rest.

Coupons

♦Cut grocery coupons from advertisements and place in a coupon holder by category and then by expiration date.
♦Keep the coupon file in your car so you will be sure to have it when shopping. Include restaurant and other discounts in a separate section in your coupon file sorted by expiration date.

Greeting Cards

♦Display your greeting cards for a few weeks from when you get them and then recycle them. Keep a few special ones in your memorabilia box or chest. Some greeting cards are nice enough to be framed. If not recycle them.

Junk Mail

♦Stop junk mail. Write on warranty cards that you do not want your name and address sold. Avoid filling out contest forms since they produce the most junk mail. Call your credit card companies and tell them you do not want your information sold.
♦Request your name to be removed from all mailing lists. It will take up to three months to see improvement.
♦Ask your postman to stop delivering junk mail or place a note by your mailboxes saying NO JUNK MAIL PLEASE.
♦Return bill enclosures and advertisement papers with your payment.

Kids Artwork

♦Set up an artwork file for each child. Keep a separate plastic hanging file box with one folder for each grade. ♦Together, with the child, select ten to twelve favourite pieces of artwork. Frame the best and hang on your wall. ♦Reduce pictures clutter by making a collage, then frame.

Letters

♦Keep favourite letters toss out the rest. Place a ribbon or elastic around the special batch and keep in your memory box for future generations to read.

Legal Papers

♦Birth, marriage, divorce and death certificates should be kept together in a fireproof safe or cabinet. House deeds, passports, stocks, bonds and other valuable papers should also be kept in this box.
♦Ask yourself, "If there was a fire and I needed to grab these files would I be able to find them?" Would they all be in one place? "If I could not get to them, would they burn in this cabinet?"

Magazines

♦Set up a holding area for current magazines. Place a large basket in your favourite reading area. Transport the basket to other reading areas in your home with ease.
♦Review magazine subscriptions regularly and cancel if they don't support your current goal in life.
♦Go through all your magazines regularly and recycle, give away to friends or donate to hospitals, doctor's offices or shelters. Magazines are always available in the library

archives.

◆Keep only favourite articles, not the whole magazine. Tear out the articles and place into your reading file and read during waiting/down times.

Newspapers
◆If the paper does not get read on the day of issue toss it out.
◆If you miss reading the paper chances are you will hear the news on Television or the Radio.
◆Clip out articles and put into your reading file then discard paper.
◆Articles are also available in libraries.
◆Read the paper online.
◆Cancel subscription if you don't read the paper every day.

School Reports/Papers
◆Group together and take photocopies of key pages, reduce the page and keep in your scrapbook.

Receipts
◆If you have too many receipts keep them in a shoebox. Sort when you have time or hire a student to do it for you on a monthly or yearly basis.
◆Use monthly hanging files for receipts. Each time you have a receipt, file by category. Total at the end of each month.

Tax Returns
◆File in a separate box and keep for seven years.

Warranties, Manuals and Instruction Books
◆Keep warranties, manuals and instruction books in a box

or in a file under the appropriate room. For example kitchen appliance warranties and operating information can be kept in the kitchen box or in an accordion file under the section named "KITCHEN".

♦File receipts and serial numbers with their manuals. Copy the receipts for tax deductible items and place the copy in the tax file for next year.

PAPER CLUTTER *General Tips*

♦Avoid buying storage containers until you eliminate excess paper clutter.

♦When setting up your ACTIVE filing system, plan on at least two to three hours to set it up. Create files in broad categories such as medical, finance, auto, health etc.

♦Keep ARCHIVE files in a remote area like the attic, garage or storage room.

♦Store valuable and legal papers in a fireproof safe or a safety deposit box.

♦Utilize the vertical space on the wall to shelve books, personal items and pictures.

♦Keep your desktop free of paperwork and other items.

♦Place an erasable message board by the phone for the entire family to use in order to cut down on paper messages. Attach an erasable marker so it will always be available.

♦Keep a spiral notebook with pen attached near the phone for messages and to make notes. Record phone numbers, addresses and other important information from incoming brochures, newsletters, city handouts, etc. in your notebook.

♦Take fifteen minutes at the end of each day to put away all papers and other items that have accumulated.

♦Keep paperwork flowing by filing, taking action and recycling. Deal with each paper you pick up.

♦Purge files regularly. Schedule a 4-6 hour appointment with yourself every six months or at least once a year.

♦Avoid paper pile up by recording the information you need into your note book and then discarding the paper.

♦Read through the next chapter on environmental clutter for ideas on how to recycle or reuse your stuff.

PAPER CLUTTER

Chapter Six

Environmental Clutter

Eliminating clutter from your life cleans up your own personal space and at the same time, promotes a healthier environment for everyone!

Getting rid of the things you don't need or use is a good way to regain control of your space, but it's only a short term solution, when you consider the bigger picture. Discarded clutter is garbage and garbage is everybody's problem. If you feel like clutter is polluting your personal space, imagine what it's doing to the environment.

Garbage in garbage out

Once your garbage is at the curbside, it becomes an environmental issue. The truck comes to take the garbage away and even though it is not in your space any more it is still your problem. Your waste, along with everyone else's, adds up to a very big heap of garbage. Once it arrives at the land-fill site, it becomes *environmental clutter.*

Everything is connected
We need to realize that all things are connected in one way or other. We are connected to each other as humans, and we are all connected to the earth. The earth is what sustains us and gives us life. It's not an understatement to say that as humans, the earth is our home. Needless to say, if earth is our home, it's our responsibility to keep it clean. We are all connected!

Are we to blame?
Everyone is so busy, just trying to make it through the day that it is easy to forget how many thoughtless decisions we make concerning our environment. We choose to drive instead of walking to the corner, we choose to eat out rather than cook for ourselves or we choose to buy a new product instead of fixing the old one. We all long for a breath of fresh air and a glass of pure water, not realizing the impact our choices make on the environment and the quality of our lives. When it comes to the depletion of our natural resources or environmental pollution it's easy to blame big industry or governments, but the fact remains, that each one of us is to blame. *Consider this - if no one sprayed their lawns with pesticide, would it still be produced?*

Manufacturing, packaging and transportation
The more we buy, the more that needs to be produced. Production requires energy, power and manufacturing

which in turn leads to pollution and waste. Toxic fumes from factory chimneys is emitted into the air and toxic waste seeps into the ground and water supply. The goods we buy are packaged and transported which in turn leads to more waste and air pollution. Once the goods reach us, we do away with the packaging, use the item a couple of times and toss it into the garbage.

Landfill Sites

Our landfill sites are filling up quickly and new sites are in demand. The problem is that no-one wants to see a dump in their backyard. Long term solutions are always being considered but there is the immediate problem of simply too much waste. Some of the waste is re-directed and recycled while some is incinerated but that still leaves tons of garbage left to decompose. There is a common misconception that stuff like paper and food easily biodegrades once it sits in the landfills. The truth is that these mountains of garbage need moisture and air to biodegrade. Recently, a dump in the USA found a newspaper that had been sitting in a site for 37 years and was still in perfect reading condition.

Did you know that paper waste accounts for 30% of most landfill while food waste accounts for the 2nd largest percentage of fill in the dumps?

Household Waste

This pie graph indicates type of waste per household per year

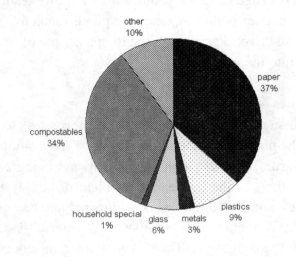

Survey was conducted in Toronto 2001. 250 Homes were surveyed for an eight week period. Single and Multiple Family units were included. This only represents a small portion of the population I believe it gives a accurate picture of what people throw out.

Did you know that landfill account for more than 30% of methane gas emissions and that methane is 20% more potent as a greenhouse gas than carbon dioxide

Toxic fumes

Garbage in a landfills produces it's own unique type of pollution. Garbage that is decomposing creates a toxic liquid called *leachate.* Some of the dumps are finding ways to collect and treat the toxic seepage. Some garbage is incinerated, but that too, creates ash, along with toxic gases such as carbon dioxide other toxic chemicals. Decomposing

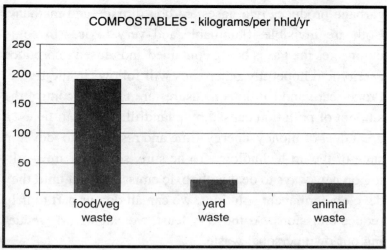

This chart represents the Compostable section of the pie graph above. As the chart indicates "food waste" ranks the highest amongst household waste.

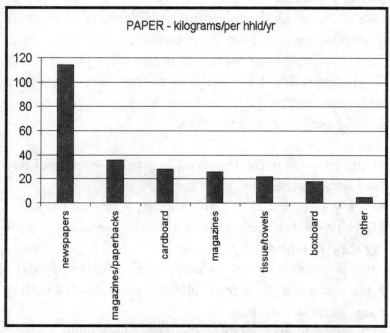

This graph represents the Paper section of the pie chart. Newspapers, followed by magazines/books are top runners in our paper waste.

107

garbage produces two gases, carbon dioxide and methane. Both are invisible, flammable and very toxic. In some dump sites the gas is being contained and reused to produce energy and hopefully other sites will follow in the future. Proper care and cautious measures are taken to control the amount of pollution caused by a landfill site but it takes a great deal of money, energy, time and resources to develop state of the art technology. To be sure, scientists are working on new ways to deal with toxic emissions, but until they develop permanent solutions, we can all do our part to help reduce emissions. At the very least, we can start by reducing our own personal waste.

Source reduction

One of the best ways to control huge amounts of waste, is to stop the garbage from being produced in the first place. This is referred to as **source reduction** or in plain English "using less stuff". Each one of us has the power to produce less waste and cut back on the garbage going to the landfills. Consider these suggestions:

♦Utilize the bulk food sections in grocery stores and buy only what you need.

♦Pack your groceries in a box or bring your own bags.

♦Give products a second life by repairing, re-using or **gifting** them to others.

♦Buy products with little or no packaging (ie bulk foods)

♦Ask cashiers to fully pack, plastic bags instead of putting a few items in each bag.

♦Complain to manufactures about over-packaging.

♦Contact your local depot about recycling guidelines and

hazardous waste disposal.

♦Compost egg shells, fruits and vegetable waste.

Recycle and Reuse

Recycling and reusing items can seriously cut down on your clutter and product waste. To learn more about recycling contact your local Waste Management Depot. Review the list below to determine how you can effectively recycle some of your clutter. Refer to the resource list in the back of the book for recycling ideas.

Automobiles

♦Consider replacing parts on your car rather then getting a new one. Learn how to fix and maintain your own car.

♦Check with local municipal government for Vehicle recycling programs. Local community colleges may also use old autos to practice on.

Furniture

♦Charitable and religious organizations are often interested in used furniture.

♦Recover when possible.

♦Sell or consign at local used furniture stores.

Paint

♦Combine leftover paints into one container and use to paint the inside of a garage or tool shed.

♦Ask neighbours and friends if they could use your leftover paint.

♦Latex paints are water based and non-toxic but alkyd paints and paint thinners contain dangerous solvents that

create vapors that are dangerous when inhaled.
♦The container may explode if crushed.
♦Do not dispose of with regular trash, take to your local hazardous waste depot.

Batteries
♦Do not dispose of household batteries with regular trash as they contain lead and sulfuric acid. Check with your local household hazardous waste depot.
♦Purchase AC/DC adapter instead of batteries or use rechargeable batteries.
♦When buying a new battery for your car, ask the station to recycle the old one.

Computers
♦Donate your old computer to local charities, women's shelters, men's shelters, youth shelters and world development agencies. Local colleges or schools may also be interested in them.
♦Check in your local yellow pages under computer recycle centers.

Eyeglasses
♦Some local pharmacies collect old glasses for organizations that send them to developing countries.
♦Call your local Institute for the Blind and inquire if they are interested.

Foam Containers
♦Foam cups, plates and trays are made from polystyrene and do not break down in landfill. Check with your local

recycle depot for guidelines for disposal.
♦Use your own reusable mugs and plates when possible.
♦ Wash and reuse paper/plastic coffee cups. (good for 3-4 uses)

Broken Glass
♦Glass is considered hazardous material and must be wrapped and labeled to protect workers from harm.

Mattresses
♦Donate your old mattress to charitable organizations. Ask the retailer if they can recycle used mattresses.

Metal
♦Scrap metal includes old air-conditioning units, hot water tanks, metal sinks, microwave ovens, aluminum siding etc.
♦Call local waste disposal for pick up dates and guidelines.

Nail Polish and Nail Polish Remover
♦Combine leftover polish together to make a new shade.
♦Unused nail polish and remover are considered hazardous waste, check with your local hazardous waste depot.

Oil
♦Car oil products can be recycled and are just as good as new when cleaned.
♦When buying, try recycled oil.

Plastics
♦Plastics are a non-renewable resource and create several pollutants when manufactured.

♦Use your own cloth bags, boxes or paper bags for groceries instead of taking plastic bags.
♦Buy strong reusable plastic containers instead of disposable ones.

Tires
♦Check with your local waste disposal depot for disposal and recycle info. Tires are ground to a powder and used for rubber floor mats and asphalt.

RECYCLE Tips

mobius loop
symbol

♦Look for the mobius loop or recycle symbol on anything you buy
♦Before tossing out stuff be sure to read over the above
♦Ask neighbours and friends if they can make use of any of your stuff before you toss it out.

♦Always check with your local Waste Management Depot for recycle guidelines

HAZARDOUS Waste
Hazardous material should **not** be put out with your regular garbage. Do not pour down the drain or dispose of improperly. These materials may cause dangerous vapors if inhaled. Below is a list of common hazardous items that can be found in almost any household.

Get a pen and check off any of the items below, that you may have in your home.

❑ Paints, paint thinner or stains
❑ Varnishes
❑ Car batteries
❑ Pesticides (fungicides, herbicide and insecticides)
❑ Aerosol containers
❑ Wood preservative
❑ Acids
❑ Lighter fluid
❑ Oven cleaner
❑ Turpentine
❑ Solvents
❑ Glues
❑ Transmission fluid
❑ Anti-freeze
❑ Photographic material
❑ Fiberglass
❑ Mothballs
❑ Disinfectant
❑ Window cleaners
❑ Pool chemicals
❑ Pharmaceutical prescriptions including syringes

Household hazardous products can be identified by the four symbols in the diagram on the next page. Always check the item *label* to determine if the product or item is dangerous to the environment or to people.

Each one of these has different degrees of danger and can be identified by the shape and then the picture inside. The Octagon Shape can be   Flammable or Toxic and the

Triangle Shape can be either Corrosive or Reactive. Check your local municipal waste disposal depot for guidelines on where and how to dispose of these items.

 Corrosive   Flammable

 Reactive   Toxic

Hazardous Products are bad for your health and the environment! Improper disposal can harm the workers, who collect your waste, filter into the ground sewage system, or ignite into flames. Some of these products can create harmful vapors. Even with an open window the vapors can get under skin and into the bloodstream. Many cases have reported that children were poisoned when they were exposed the the vapors. Hazardous material should be properly labeled and never mixed together with each other. When possible, try to use alternatives for household cleaning.

I am a mother of four children, ranging in ages from one to ten. I live in a fairly upscale neighbourhood with homes sporting beautiful landscaping and perfectly manicured lawns. This spring while I was enjoying a lovely walk with my children I took note of a sign on a lawn that I had seen many times in the past. It was a sign indicating that the owners had sprayed the lawn with pesticides. The sign had a red slash suggesting that this was considered a danger for children and animals. I remember asking myself if a few weeds were worth poisoning children and animals. Suddenly I felt sick to my stomach. I too, was guilty of putting this pesticide on my lawn. Last year I remember the cat getting sick, meanwhile all I was only thinking about having a great looking lawn. By the time I got home from my walk I had decided that I would not be using that poison on my lawn ever again. I talked my husband into doing it the old fashioned way, by seeding properly. The funny thing is that our lawn has become the talk of the street. Everyone was asking how we did it , and I gladly told them that I certainly did not spray with pesticides. I think I started a trend in my neighbourhood. I feel good that I am doing something to help clean up the environment if only in my own front yard.

Lidia K. - Richmond Hill Ontario

ALTERNATIVES

There are many alternatives other than using toxic chemicals in your home. Here are just a few inexpensive toxic free ideas for your home.

Oven

Clean your oven while still warm. Make a paste using baking soda and water and use steel wool or cleaning brush to scrub the oven.

Toilet

Mix ½ cup of baking soda in a small amount of water and scrub with toilet brush. White vinegar also works well in

CLUTTER CUTTER GUIDE

the toilet bowl. Borax mixed with vinegar also works as a disinfectant.

Drains

Mix ½ cup of baking soda with hot water and ½ cup of vinegar. Use a plunger and flush your drains with the mixture regularly.

Windows

Use white vinegar and newspapers to clean glass and windows. Water with a little soap and a squeegee brush also work great on windows.

TIPS

♦Buy cleaners that are environmentally safe. Check the symbols and read the labels.

♦Purchase only goods that are recycled and that can be recycled again.

♦Make your own cleaners with natural products.

♦Buy only what you need.

♦Try to use one multi purpose cleaner for everything.

♦Avoid pouring chemical cleaners down sinks or drains.

♦Check your local Hazardous Waste Depot for disposal instructions on how to properly dispose of dangerous products.

Partial School Speech given by a grade 5 student
Feb 2002
Edited and shortened

The Danger Zone
By Robert, age 10

Everyday my family feels like we have to cross a highway to get to school. Cars are parked everywhere and cars are zooming in all directions. It is a very dangerous situation. I have seen some students run across the road and parking lot and nearly get hit by a car. I see drivers parking in the wrong spots everyday. This is not only illegal but it is also very dangerous for pedestrians. While parents wait to pick up their kids they park everywhere including in front of fire hydrant. Blocking a fire hydrant is dangerous. If there was an emergency and the fire fighters needed to use it the fire hydrant would be blocked and fire fighters would not be able to see it. When there is a fire, every second counts.

Cars also park on the school driveway and even when they wait on the side of the street they still block pedestrians and traffic. Most of the cars are Mini Vans so when they park it makes it hard to see when you cross the street.

I am also worried about the air pollution from those big cars. Sometimes parents sit in their car with the engine still running. I know that breathing in those fumes is not good for our health especially if there are lots of cars with their engines running at the same time.

Students who live close to our school should consider walking to school. It is a healthier choice and it can help solve the problem of too many vehicles crowded around the school. Walking is good for the environment, good for your health and it is very good exercise.

117

Chapter Seven

Simplify and Be Free!

Life is a rush

Material possessions or stuff doesn't seem to be making us happy any more. Things have gone out of balance. We are working too many hours, doing too many things, spending less time with our loved ones and have lost touch with nature. We have big homes filled with lots of stuff, we have toys to play with, the newest and best machines and computers and we drive big shiny cars.

We rush around trying to make ends meet just so we can keep up this lifestyle that we have grown accustomed to. The more we buy the more we work the less time we have. The less time we have the faster we run trying to get things done. We eat fast, drive fast, work fast. As a result we are not eating right, not spending quality time with our families and getting deeper into debt. There are so many fast food outlets to choose from and if we want to eat at home we buy pre-cooked frozen food entree. We buy products that promise to make things more efficient, faster, and easier. We are conditioned to believe that we should have what we want right away because we deserve it. No money, no problem, the bank is quick to lend us money and give us credit cards so we can pre-spend our money.

Feeling out-of-control?

One day you wake up feeling like you are on a never ending merry-go-round and wonder just when it will stop and let you off. You have everything and yet you still feel empty, stressed out and unhappy. You lay back turn on the TV to watch the morning news and then before your very eyes, the answer to all your problems "Are you feeling tired, stressed and out-of-control, we've got the answer, the new and improved XYZ Electronic Daytimer, only $199.99 plus shipping and handling "have your credit card ready and order today!" You pick up the phone take out the credit card and place the order. "Well that was simple." you say, and then up you get, take a quick shower, grab a quick bite, get into your big new car, grind your way through the worst traffic jam of your life. You arrive at work and struggle through another busy day, just waiting for it to end. You rush home pick up your kids and drop one off to their game and then off you go to the mall. Finally, you make your way home, cook a quick meal, pay some bills, watch TV and go to bed. You drift off to sleep dreaming about the long weekend that's coming up, when you will finally get to

SIMPLIFY AND BE FREE

go to the cottage. This year you are going to leave at 4 in the morning hoping to miss the traffic. Maybe this year you can make it in 4 hours instead of five (amazing isn't it - you are even getting stressed in your dreams). Before you know it it's time to get up again.

"Buying stuff and accumulating possessions does not pave the road to happiness it clutters up the lane to freedom."

Get out of Debt

How did life get so complicated? There has got to be a better way. We work hard to make money but no matter how much we make, it is still not enough. Perhaps we need to take a good look at what we are spending our money on. The excess accumulation of stuff in your home should be a clear indication of where you have been spending your money. Think about it. If you were willing to get rid of just one quarter of your clutter you would not need as much space, which would mean that you could live in a smaller home. Take a look at all of the things that are costing you money. Things like cars you don't use. My friend has a little red sports car in his garage called a "Spyder". He stores it, washes it, insures it and hardly ever drives it. I don't remember the last time he actually drove it. He claims to have taken it around the block a few times. Last I heard, his insurance was costing him a pretty penny. I think the car itself is worth a small mortgage. He is always complaining about being in debt, yet, he never entertains the idea of selling it. There is a number of other interesting ways you can save money and get out of debt. I suggest you pick up a copy of the book called "Your Money or Your Life" written by Joe Dominguez and Vickie Robins. The book has some simple, yet doable ways of cutting back and saving money, without having to drastically change you life.

People are looking to find ways of simplifying their lives so they can have the freedom to do things they love. Freedom and simplicity mean different things to different people.

For me freedom is being able to take a weekend off and spend time at home doing simple things like making a home cooked meal for my family and spending time in my flower garden.
Margaret, age 56 Nurse

Cutting the clutter
Removing the clutter, forces you to take a look at your stuff and face some pretty hard facts. You find yourself shaking your head and asking questions like. "Do these things make me happy? Am I still paying for this? What a waste, I've never used it, why did I buy it?" Once you get past the guilt, frustration of your "possession obsession" you will begin to take back control of your life. Your stuff will no longer hold you captive. Sorting through your clutter and getting rid of stuff is a a big step towards freedom. The next big step is to keep it from coming back into your life. You need to free yourself from consumerism.

Freedom from consumerism
Commercials have played a huge part in keeping us hungry for more. We are told what we need and we comply and run out and buy, buy, buy. It's second nature to us. We see, we

want and we buy. Advertising fuels consumerism and is controlled by corporations so the more you consume, the more money they make and the more products they produce. The need for the product is created and sold to you along with the goods. We need to think before we run out and buy things. Getting away from consumerism is another way of taking control of your life. You need to decide for yourself whether or not you need something. Commercials create a desire for you to acquire and try to convince you that you need the product that it will make you happy.

My favourite thing is playing computer games. As soon as a new one comes out I get my parents to get it for me. It's easy cause they have lots of credit cards and stuff and they just call and order it. Sometimes my uncle buys them for me because he is the coolest. If I don't play the video games I get bored. My friends come over cause I have lots of cool games. I get all the best games first because my dad has a satellite dish and we get all the best channels and I get to see lots of commercials before anyone else does. **Albert, age 9**

Once I saw something on TV and I asked my mom to buy it. The commercial said it would spin around for five minutes and that it did all kinds of neat tricks and stuff. I begged my mom to buy it for me. Finally she bought it for me and I was so happy. I tried to make it work the way the TV said but it didn't work hardly at all. I was upset because they lied and showed the kids laughing and playing with it for a long time. Ever since that time I don't believe anything they show on TV because they just want you to buy it. Now when I see something I want to see it work first so I go to the store to try it out before I buy it. Sometimes it is good and other times it is just junk. **Charles age 10**

It's a sad thing to see how commercials are being targeted to kids. It seems that commercials are better than some of the TV shows or movies. I remember a friend of mine saying that the only reason she watches the Super Bowl is because she loves the commercials and so do her children. Not only do we have to deal with our own personal desire to acquire possessions we comply to our children's' every day demands to purchase products for them. They are just going with the flow and asking for what everyone else is getting and just trying to keep up with their friends. Children just want to be normal and normal to them is owning the right stuff. The right stuff helps them fit into a group. I once heard a teenager say to another. "Let's party with Joe, he's a geek but that's ok, he drives Mustang and has lots of cool stuff at his place"

I personally don't follow any clothing fads or buy the newest and best stuff. Most of my time and effort goes into sports. I find that spending my time and energy in sports helps me stay away from the shopping malls. I have friends that go shopping almost every day. Some times they even skip classes to go buy shoes and stuff. Their parents give them cash whenever they want and often you will see them with credit cards or bank cards. I don't think they even think twice about spending $200 in one day. The most important thing to them is to look great and wear the newest and best stuff so they can be with the in crowd. What bothers me is that they only wear things a few times and they are off buy-

ing more stuff. Maybe their parents have lots of cash. In my school people look at you funny if you say you bought a pair of shoes for only $10. or if you wear stuff that you buy in a discount store. **Josette T Age 15**

The best stuff in life is not stuff

The acquisition of possessions has complicated our lives so much that all we seem to be doing is running around buying and looking for things that promise to make us happy. We learn very quickly that things can only bring temporary happiness. Once we get bored with our stuff we start looking for the next thing that promises to make us more happy than the last.

We constantly rush around looking for things to make us happy that we seldom realize how much time we invest in ***things rather than people***. It's a fact that we spend so little time with our family that most children grow up in front of the TV or at the Mall.

Ask yourself these questions, each and every time you are compelled to go out and buy. Print these questions and carry them around with you until the routine becomes second nature to you. Ask yourself:
1. Do I need it?
2. Do I want it?
3. Can I afford it? How much will it really cost me? Does it have to be dry cleaned? If it breaks can I fix it?
4. Am I willing and do I have time to maintain it?
5. How long will it last? Is it good quality?
6. Is it something that I can borrow or rent?

7. Is it made from recycled material and when we are ready to dispose of it, can it be recycled?
8. Does it have toxic materials, will it pollute the environment and is it hazardous?
9. How and where and by whom is the product made?
10. Before you decide to run out and buy something why not give yourself a few days "cooling off period". If you still want it ask yourself those questions again.

What is Simplicity
Merriam Webster's Dictionary Definition
Simple Uncomplicated, unassuming or unpretentious, free from elaboration, readily understood

If you look up the word simple in the dictionary you will find lines and lines of meaning for simple. In the context of this book I have chosen the description that applies to simplifying life. Still the word simple can mean different things to different people. However, there is one thing that most dictionary definitions would agree with and that is that simple means uncomplicated. Certainly we can all agree that we are leading a life that is a far cry from simple.

My idea of simplicity is living in a small town or community where everyone says hello to you. A place where you can walk on the sidewalk or ride your bike without having to worry about traffic or air pollution. I would buy my fresh produce from a local farmer, shopping at the small grocery store on the corner, and buy homemade jam from lady next door. Simplicity is getting away from traffic jams, shopping malls and flashy billboards. - **Jane, Age 47 Teacher**

Living a healthy and balanced life

I believe that the trend is going more towards living a simple, healthy and balanced life. We all are looking to free ourselves from debt, work less hours and spend more time with our friends and families. Working less and living more is something worth striving for and we can all attain this if are willing to cut back on the desire to buy and consume more than what we need.

Simplicity to me is having one day a week, like Sunday, as a day off so that we can spend time with our families. Family dinners seem to be going out of style these days. I think that six days a week is enough for any human being to work. Everything should be closed on Sunday that way there would be no excuse for families not to be together. Life is too complicated that is why I believe that having one day a week off would simplify life for everyone.- **Richard age 53, Leasing Sales Manager**

Our lives have become easier but certainly not simpler. What would we do without the modern conveniences that we have become so used to? Like fast cars and jets to help us get there faster, fax machines, telephones and computers to help us communicate faster or drugs to help us heal? What would happen if we didn't have water, electricity or air conditioning? And of course what if there were not grocery stores or malls? Where would we shop for food or clothing? What if there were no shopping malls? What would we do on the weekend, where would we send the kids? The thought of having to go back to a time where we didn't have all of these modern conveniences seems downright terrifying.

To sustain life we need basics like water, food, shelter, clothing, electricity and transportation. We have gone above and beyond what we need to what we want and must have no matter what the cost. The end result is that our pocket book, our health, our family, our community and our planet is being drastically affected by our attitude towards our possessions and our over consumption of goods. We have become so obsessed with possessions that it has dominated our very existence.

Lately there have been many books and websites dedicated to the idea of getting away from commercialism and moving towards a more simple way of living. Simplified living promotes a more humane way of living. I suggests that we shift our attitude towards materialism and consumerism and take a good look at the things in life that really matter. There are groups, organizations and entire communities dedicated to this new way of living. The information and the brilliance of some of the people involved in this movement will give you insight and inspire you to make changes towards a more human existence on this planet. Refer to the recommended reading section at the back of the book for an updated list of books and websites on the subject.

Most people who are looking to simplify their life do so for the following reasons;
♦Freedom from debt
♦Harmony and balance in their lives
♦Desire to re-connect with nature

♦Control careless spending on impulse items and disposable goods

♦Buy quality goods that have a longer life span

♦Recycle as much as possible and to consume as little as possible

♦Respect for the environment by not buying or using hazardous or toxic goods

♦Re-evaluate and re-instate family and community values

♦Non-materialistic ways of celebrating holidays and life

Living a simple lifestyle does not mean that you need to move into a cabin in the woods, unplug yourself from the grid, dig your own well, grow your own vegetables and become a recluse. Although I do know a couple that have been doing that for the past 10 years and they are living a wonderful and fulfilled life. Living a simple lifestyle is about freeing yourself from the strings of materialism and living on purpose. It is about making choices and not allowing your self to be controlled by the consumerism machine.

Living off the Land

(translated from Italian) When we came to Canada we had so much to be thankful for. All we had was the shirts on our back and a couple of dollars. We lived with friends for a while, and worked hard then we bought a very small house with a nice little piece of land. The land was more important than the house. My wife and I worked day and night getting the land ready for planting. We planted lots of vegetables, mostly tomatoes. In the fall we picked and saved everything. My wife made tomato sauce and put them in jars. We dried out lots of the vegetables and froze as much

as we could. Our neighbour had a freezer and he let us keep our food in there for us. In the winter we had lots of food to

eat. We made soup and sauces out of the tomatoes, ate lots of beans, baked bread and we never starved. It's been 48 years since I came to this country and I still grow my vegetable garden and my wife still makes tomato sauce. I have seven children who are all grown now. I worked hard on the railroad and clearing bushes and my wife stayed home and took care of the kids. Still I was always able to pay the bills, and provide food and shelter for my family. The kids are all grown up now and have families of

their own. Thankfully a few of the kids have learned how to plant vegetables and make tomato sauce for themselves. This is good because no matter what, I know that if they know how to grow a good garden and make home made bread they will never go hungry.

Mario, age 76 retired

Planting a vegetable garden is one of the most simple yet rewarding things you can do. It doesn't take much time, saves you money and most of all, it feels so natural.

it. Remember things cost, time, money and space.

How do you spend your Time?
by David Leonhardt, a.k.a. The Happy Guy

Somebody is robbing you blind.

· *Tick. Tick. Tick.*

Somebody is stealing you most precious possession.

Tick. Tick. Tick.

You will never recover what has been taken away.

Tick Tick Tick.

Time. Time is finite. Once we use it, we lose it. And every minute we spend chasing after money is a minute stolen away. Does money get in the way of your life? Silly question, of course it does. It also helps you enjoy your life. The question should be, "Does the pursuit of money consume too much of your time?"

The top four ways to tell if money is consuming too much of your time

1.   You sleep on the job because if you didn't you would have to sleep on one of your other jobs.

2.   You buy a new car because a neighbor just did ... for the third time this week.

3.   Your mother calls, but you are busy on the Internet watching stocks move. You ask her to call back next year.

4.   You want Christmas declared a public nuisance because banks and stock markets are closed.

Amazingly enough, as our standard of living has increased over our lifetime, happiness indicators have not. It turns out that happiness is more about quality of time and relationships than about quantity of "stuff" we store in our brick and wood boxes we call houses.

Money doesn't buy happiness, but the lack of money can drive people into complete misery. When times get tight, stress levels shoot through the roof. But what does "tight" mean?

Most people have never seen "tight." Imagine the horror of having to cut back from two movie rentals a week to one. Or going to war against Iraq or Afghanistan or some other enemy-of-the-hour and -- get this -- soldiers die. It's true! Not just one, but several. Whod-a-thunk?

The simple fact is that if someone took away half of everything I own, I would still be rich. And if someone took away half of what was left, I would still be rich. And if that was halved once more, I would still be rich.

Most of our spending, including much of our housing, transportation, food and clothing is discretionary. We don't need new clothes; we can buy them used. We don't

132

need a house; apartments are available. We don't need a
new or big car, just something that runs most of the time.
We don't need pre-cooked dinners full of deadly preserva-
tive. These are things we want, not things we need. When
they come to take away your TV ... then panic!

What we need to be happy is to appreciate what we have -
- the stuff, the people, the experiences, the knowledge --
rather than crave and long for what we lack.

Oh no! Not another top-four list.

So, here are The Happy Guy's top four tips for getting
over our addiction to money through appreciation:

1.   Walk around your house for five minutes each day.
Look at things you usually take for granted. Imagine what
life would be like if they were not there. Appreciate them.
(If you realize life would not be any worse without the
object, you probably have a clutter problem, and this book
can help!)

2.   Say grace at dinner every day. Even if you do not
believe in God, thank somebody for something that hap-
pened that day.

3.   Start a gratitude journal. Why not write down
things you appreciate? Some people can feel it more that
way.

4.   Call somebody up and say, "Thank you for being

in my life. You have made it richer. I enjoy you. Thank you."

Thank you for reading this. You have made my life richer. (See I'm rich no matter how little money I have.)

The author is David Leonhardt, author of Climb your Stairway to Heaven: the 9 habits of maximum happiness. Visit him at www.TheHappyGuy.com

Guidelines to Simplify and Be Free

1. Live on Purpose. Review your goals and never bring things into your life that do not support your goals. What are your priorities in life, family, job and health? Keep only things that support your goals and priorities.

2. Place value on space, time and money. Put a price on your time and ask yourself if the item you're investing in will cost you time and money in maintaining it as well as upkeep. Put a price on the square footage of your space. How much will it cost you to store this item? Are you certain you will have the time to use it?

3. Set Boundaries and limitations. How much is enough. Enforce the one in and one out rule. One junk drawer, one scrapbook, one container of plastic bags, one bookcase, one toy box, etc.

4. Shop Wisely. Never go shopping when you're hungry and never shop on impulse. If you have the impulse to buy something you don't really need, write it down and leave it for a week and if you still want it after a week reconsider buying it but ask yourself how it will serve your goals and priorities and what are you willing to let go if you purchase

5. Swap before you buy. Swap clothing, tools, and books before going out and buying them. Join a swap and barter club.

6. Borrow before you buy. Go to your library and borrow books, magazines and videos or ask friends and neighbours if you can borrow rather than buying something you may only use once. Try out a friends exercise bike for a few days before you decide to buy one.

7. Rent "costly" equipment before you decide to buy it.

8. Give consumable gifts such as food coupons, show passes, massage therapy certificates, manicures and oil changes. They are more appreciated than stuff.

9. Group gift giving and **drawing names** is an alternative to Christmas gift buying madness.

10. Be charitable with stuff you no longer need.

11. Don't be Victim to commercials. Commercials are designed to make you feel that you need their product whether or not you need them. Turn off the TV

12. Teach your children about the consumerism monster

13. Say No to junk mail and ask to be removed from mailing lists and useless subscriptions. You can find what you need online, in newspapers or libraries.

14. Buy locally and support your community

15. Grow you own vegetable garden.

Once you start cutting back on the stuff you buy you will accumulate less clutter and save money. Your values will change and the knowledge that you gain by carefully choosing what you bring into your home and what you throw out will help you get away from consumerism.

In conclusion remember that cutting the clutter is easy. The challenge is to keep it from coming back into your life. Freedom comes from making conscious choices and being aware of what you value in life. Nothing says it better than the following quote.

"What is freedom? Freedom is the right to choose: the right to create for yourself the alternatives of choice. Without the possibility of choice and the exercise of choice a man is not a man but a member, an instrument, a thing."
- Archibald MacLeish

SIMPLIFY AND BE FREE

Recommended Reading

Other Books by Lina Visconti
Seven Step Feng Shui and Feng Shui, Going With The Flow
Simply Feng Shui, The Art of Placement - Video

Websites
www.fengshuican.com and www.linavisconti.com

Contact
Lina Visconti c/o TM Publications
9251-8 Yonge Street #121
Richmond Hill, Ontario, Canada L4C 9T3
Tel: 416-336-8666 or email lina@fengshuican.com

More Suggested Reading
The Power of Place *by Winifred Gallagher*
Your Money or Your Life, *Joe Dominguez &Vickie Robin*
Climb your Stairway to Happiness, *by David Leonhardt*
Who Will Cry When You Die? *by Robin Sharma*
Office Clutter and Clutters Last Stand *by Don Aslett*
Life, Energy and The Emotions *by John Diamond*

Websites to visit
www.simpleplanet.com
www.simpleliving.net

Resources

1-800-GOT-JUNK
Website: www.1-800-gotjunk.com
Service provided throughout North America
hey pick up your junk for disposal.

Recycling Council of Ontario
Website: www.web.net/rco
489 College Street, Suite 504
Toronto, Ontario
Phone: (416) 960-1025
A non-profit, charitable organization. They reduce need-
less waste. Promotes reduction, reuse and recycling.

Ministry of Environment and Energy (M.O.E.E.)
Public Information Centre
135 St Clair Avenue West
Toronto, Ontario
Phone: (416) 325-4000
This organization deals with waste management in
Ontario. The public information centre provides general
information on the 3R's.

Re-Uze Building Centre
1210 Birchmount Avenue, Unit 1A
Scarborough, Ontario M1P 2C3
Phone: (416) 750-4000
This organization sells new and used building materials
for commercial and residential properties.

Goodwill Industries
234 Adelaide Street East
Toronto, Ontario M5A 1M9
Phone: (416) 362-4711
This is a non-profit organization that recycles and sells donated clothing, furniture and appliances.

St Vincent De Paul Society
240 Church Street
Toronto, Ontario
Phone: (416) 740-9595
This is a non-profit organization. They provide social service programs by selling donated items. They have home for deaf children, recovering alcoholics, mentally handicapped people and street people.

Salvation Army Family Services
100 Lombard Street
Toronto, Ontario
Phone: (416) 366-4686
Operates social services funded by sale of donated items.

Canadian National Institute for the Blind (CNIB)
320 McLeod Street
Ottawa, Ontario
Phone: (613) 563-4021

R.A.G.S. (Reusing Articles for Global Survival)
2084 Walkley Road
Ottawa, Ontario
Phone: (613) 739-4857

Bibliography

Gaia's Body, Volk, Tyler,
C- COPERNICUS, 1998
ISBN# 0-387-98270-1

Earthmind, Devereux, Paul
Destiny Books, 1992.
ISBN# 0-89281-367-9

Love The Life You Love, Sher, Barbara,
DTP- Dell Trade Paperback, March 1997
ISBN# 0-440-50756-1

Sacred Space, Linn, Denise
Great Britain Random House, 1995
ISBN# 0-345-39769-X

Good News For A Change, Suzuki, David
Lockwood, Georgene,
STODDART, 2002
ISBN# 0-7737-3307-8

Organizing Your Life-(Complete Idiot's Guide)
Lockwood, Georgene,
alpha books, 1999.
ISBN# 0-02-863382-2

The New Natural House Book, Pearson, David, Fireside
Simon & Schuster, 1998.
ISBN# 0-684-84733-7

Clear your Clutter with Feng Shui, Kingston, Karen
Broadway, Judy Piatkus Publishers, Great Britain 1998.
ISBN# 0-7679-0359-5

House as a Mirror of Self, Marcus, Clair Cooper
Conari Press, 1995.
ISBN# 1-57324-076-1

Lighten Up, Passoff, Michelle,
Harper Perennial, 1998.
ISBN# 0-06-095265-2

Seven Step Feng Shui, Visconti, Lina,
TM Publications Worldwide, 1998.
ISBN# 0-9684391-0-1

Going with the Flow, Visconti, Lina,
TM publications Worldwide, 1999.
ISBN# 0-9684391-1-X

The Simple Living Guide, Luhrs, Janet
Dell Publishing Group, 1997.
ISBN# 0-555-06796-6

Living the Simple Life, St James, Elain
Hyperion, New York 1996.
ISBN# 0-7868-6219-X

Simplify Your Life, St James, Elain,
Hyperion, New York 1994.
ISBN# 0-7868-8000-7

Voluntary Simplicity, Elgin, Duane
Quill William Morrow, New York 1981.
ISBN# 0-688-12119-5

Your Money or Your Life,
Dominguez, Joe and Vickie Robin
Viking, New York 1992.
ISBN# 0-670-84331-8